P9-DFO-633

No. 1294
$10.95

CHAIN SAWS: BUYING, USING, MAINTAINING, REPAIRING

BY ROBERT A. OUELLETTE

TAB **TAB BOOKS Inc.**

BLUE RIDGE SUMMIT, PA. 17214

FIRST EDITION

FIRST PRINTING

Copyright © 1981 by TAB BOOKS Inc.

Printed in the United States of America

Reproduction or publication of the content in any manner, without express permission of the publisher, is prohibited. No liability is assumed with respect to the use of the information herein.

Library of Congress Cataloging in Publication Data

Ouellette, Robert A.
   Chainsaws : buying, using, maintaining, repairing.

   Includes index.
   1. Chain saws. I. Title.
TJ1233.09   621.9'3   81-9165
ISBN 0-8306-0013-2   AACR2
ISBN 0-8306-1294-7 (pbk.)

Preface

An acquaintance of mine recently asked how long it took me to write this book. My reply to him was "27 years." This book is the culmination of my entire career in the chain saw repair business. I began to consider putting this kind of a manual together 10 years ago. I recognized the need for such a book because of the great many chain saws being bought. In the past year or so, I realized that this kind of information is now in the "necessity" category. Many of the saws purchased in recent years have come back to me for so many repairs that could be done by the owners.

If there was any one thing that pushed me into completing this book, it was the knowledge that there were more than 100,000 recorded injuries due to chain saw kickback alone in 1979.

I have attempted to write this book with the occasional user in mind rather than making it a manual for repairmen or the professional users. The large majority of saws are being sold to the occasional user. Professional loggers are capable of performing the repairs as I have set them forth in this book and repairmen are in need of a more extensive set of manuals that make reference to each and every brand and model of saw. However, I would be quite flattered if either of these latter categories of people were to find this material useful to them.

This book could have been double the size and still not covered the entire subject. It could also have been far briefer and might have treated the subject satisfactorily. I chose this format because it has proven to be a valid concept for me over the years. I set it forth this way with the confidence that it will be just as valid for the reader.

My advice is based on information gained by close association with saw and component designers, manufacturers of saws and saw chain, loggers, foresters, maintenance engineers, and safety engineers. By seeking out and using all available information gained personally in this manner, I intend to provide the reader with the most complete guide ever written to the practical and safe use of chain saws.

Contents

DEDICATION

To Major T. Benton, past director of Laughing Brook Wildlife Sanctuary and Educational Center, Hampden, Massachusetts, for his encouragement, guidance and editorial skills, which have made all of this possible.

BEATITUDES OF A CHAIN SAW REPAIR SHOP

Blessed is he who borroweth or loaneth his chain saw, for he provideth me with many repairs.

Blessed art thou who purchaseth from discount stores, for they payeth me for set-ups and advice.

Blessed art ye who useth cheap motor oils, for ye giveth to me motors to repair.

Blessed are thee, who refuseth to use chain & bar oils, for ye maketh me bars to rebuild.

Blessed art thou who cutteth into roots, nails and dirt, for ye buyeth from me many new chains.

Blessed are thou who continueth to runneth dirty saws, for ye delivereth to me many unnecessary tune-ups.

Blessed art thee who continueth to run dull chains, for ye truly keepeth me in business.

Introduction

A little philosophy! There perhaps has never been developed a portable cutting tool as efficient as the chain saw! Designed and developed to cut through 12-inch diameter hardwood logs at the rate of 1-inch per second, the modern chain saw is the ultimate in a cutting instrument. Unfortunately, it will also cut legs, hands, arms and even faces at a more rapid rate.

Unlike almost any other portable cutting tool, such as Skil saws, table saws, and band saws that have at least a portion of their cutting blades covered by guards and covers, the chain saw's cutting edges are totally exposed. By current design, it must be this way. But simply because of this fact, the chain saw can be one of the most dangerous tools a person will take into their hands.

As dangerous as a chain saw is, anyone, regardless of age, sex, physical strength or mental capability can purchase these exacting tools from any kind of outlet—from discount stores and catalog showrooms to hardware stores and servicing power equipment dealers—and receive *not one word of caution* about the potential dangers to which they are about to subject themselves. They will be told nothing about the correct method of felling a tree or of bucking up the tree.

Complete novices are assumed to be capable of dropping trees of considerable size and weight from day one and with no anticipated incidence of injury to themselves, their companions or damage to property surrounding them. I find such a void of safety instructions to be beyond comprehension and I fear that the day is fast approaching when such safety measures will be mandatorily imposed upon the industry by government agencies. I hope the industry will initiate the necessary measures to make the chain saw a safer product long before we allow this to occur.

If this book prevents one injury it will have fulfilled its purpose and justified my efforts.

Since the energy crisis of 1973, the chain saw industry has undergone a dramatic change. Once considered to be the exclusive tool of lumbering and forestry related industries, the continuing energy crisis has transformed the chain saw from a tool of the professionals to the salvation of the individual home owner.

From sales of a little over 1 million units in 1972, the chain saw industry is now producing over 5 million units a year. Better than 3 million of these saws will find their way into the hands of the home owner—the occasional user. Faced with continually rising fuel costs, people across America are outfitting themselves to provide firewood as a supplement or replacement for their costly conventional heating systems.

Two of the most visible results of the blackmail being fostered on the American public by the OPEC nations and their henchmen are the high costs of gasoline to run our automobiles and the prices being demanded for home heating oils. Both commodities doubled in cost in just one year. This left us helpless to do much short of utilizing public transportation, car-pooling, and producing gasahol and other energy alternatives. However, we do have a means to achieve at least a sense of independence by providing ourselves with a method of heating our homes—while in effect thumbing our noses at the cartels that are driving our living costs right out of sight—and that means the chain saw!

The chain saw has come of age as a valuable and practical tool. As I drive throughout the New England countryside, I observe more homes with woodpiles nearby than those that do not have woodpiles. Even city dwellers have been installing wood stoves as a means of heating independence.

Simply owning a chain saw does not make us "independent" because the ownership of a saw is not free of involvement. The saw does require fuel to run it and there are considerable maintenance demands. There are chains to sharpen, bars to maintain, starters to rewind, clutches, ignitions, and so on. The chain saw, in reality, is a very high-maintenance item. Additionally, there is the ever-persistent problem of finding a source of wood.

Beyond all these problems, there is a very real safety concern with the use of chain saws. As more and more saws find their way into the hands of novices, more and more saw-related accidents are being recorded—and even a considerable number of deaths! It is estimated that one user in six will be involved in some sort of chain saw related accident each year. Accidents range from a simple back strain from over-extending our poorly conditioned bodies to the more serious type injuries caused by chain saw kickback or being struck by falling trees and branches. As the use of the chain-saw increases, so does the risk of injury. And as more saws are marketed, the more maintanance will be required.

In my opinion, there is no other adequate manual available for the first-time chain saw purchaser which will tell you how to maintain the saw correctly and completely. With the exception of the few incidental paragraphs provided in the owners' manuals that are provided with some saws, there is not one satisfactory reference guide available dealing with the dangers involved in using a chain saw or the correct methods for dropping a tree.

In all my 27 years in the chain saw business, I have been unable to provide a customer with a reliable and complete reference covering all the necessary aspects of safe chain saw use. While it is true that owners' manuals have given more attention to safety in recent years, I still believe they do not go far enough in instructing a novice about the potential dangers inherent in chain saw usage. They do not give much advice about the safe and correct manner of using a saw in a woodlot. In my estimation, most manuals are woefully inadequate when it comes to a practical guide to chain saw maintenance.

For the potential purchaser of a chain saw, there is no real guide to go by that will tell the whole story. Surely there are buyer's guides available, but they just don't get into the real guts of what chain saw to buy. Most such guides are authored by persons outside the profession and can't approach the real technical aspects of saws. They are mostly specification comparisons and they leave a lot to be desired.

Based on my experience in this industry for more than a quarter of a century, I will make qualified comparisons and recommendations in this book in a way I have found to be valid for my thousands of customers. In the chapters that follow, I will guide you concerning the purchase of a saw, the care and maintenance of the unit, safety tips, methods for managing a woodlot, and the dangerous aspects of chain saw use.

Chapter 1

The History of the Chain Saw

As with most inventions, it would be difficult to pinpoint exactly when the "chain saw" was created. Certainly as long as man has gathered wood he undoubtedly dreamed of using some easier, mechanical means to simplify the chore. These dreams first started to come together in 1858; it was then that the first United States patent was issued to Harvey Brown of New York City for what was called an "endless sectional sawing mechanism." This device was nothing more than a band saw with a series of hinged sections riding on hexagonal pulleys.[1]

In 1863, the second chain saw patent was issued to George Kammerl of New York City. Mr. Kammerl's invention was entitled "Improvement in Endless Saws," and consisted of a "saw blade that is formed of a number of tempered steel plates or links firmly held together by rivets to form an endless chain, the outside edge of which carries the required teeth adapted to cutting wood, or other material, this whole chain or chain saw blade moving continuously in one single direction over a system of grooved pulleys, one or more of which receive the required motive power . . . The amount of wood actually cut away may be greater than in ordinary known saws, although it rarely need be more than three-eighth of an inch."[2]

---

[1]Miller, Charles I., "History of Chain Saws," Department of Forestry and Conservation, Purdue University, Lafayette, Indiana, from *Southern Lumberman*, issue of April 15, 1949.

[2]*Ibid.*

While these two inventions were forerunners of our modern methods of cutting wood with chain saws, it took many years to progress beyond that point. Between 1863 and 1905, there were at least 12 more patents issued for machinery described as improvements on existing methods of the day. However, they all had one thing in common. All of them ignored any mention of a method for powering their devices. All of this thinking could not get beyond the theoretical stage simply because there was no known means of power light enough to be used with a portable saw.

Whether or not these inventors had intended their designs to be portable or stationary is not mentioned. In this respect, all of the foregoing falls into what I refer to as phase I of the chain saw history: the idealistic and theoretical hopes of man to cut wood by mechanical means.

POTLATCH MACHINE

Phase II of chain saw history is divided into two categories. First, there were the crude attempts at powered wood cutting as evolved in 1906 when the Potlatch Lumber Company of Potlatch, Idaho, installed a crude log deck chain saw in their mill. They used this machinery for several years. This creation was an improvement of a workable mechanical chain saw built by the Ashland Iron Works of Ashland, Oregon and powered by compressed air. The compressed air design was actually used by the Scott and Van Arsdale Company of California. After a short trial period, it was found not to be workable. The Potlatch machine worked for a period of time, but it was never patented.

In 1908 Mr. Charles Wolf saw the possibilities in the Potlatch device and created a more efficient saw that was installed at the Blackwell Lumber Company in Couer D'Alene, Idaho. Mr. Wolf neglected to patent his invention even though it was produced in limited quantities by the Union Iron Works of Spokane, Washington.

For the next 15 years, Mr. Wolf constructed and marketed successful chain saws powered by electric motors. They weighed as much as 90 pounds, utilized 4-foot bars and had chains that looked much like the two-cutter tooth cross-cut saws we know of today. Ineffective as it might sound, there was one advantage to it. When it became dulled travelling in one direction, it was simply reversed and would cut in the other direction. While effective to a point, the Wolf saw did not fulfill the needs of the logging industry and was eventually discarded.

A significant point was reached in the 1920s. It was in these years that mechanical geniuses throughout the world were developing the internal combustion engine and patenting numerous inventions related to it. As the performances improved, the weights kept falling to more acceptable levels. At last the world could attach one of these engines to the mechanical devices already developed! Although it appeared to be simple enough, there was still a great deal of perserverance required by these mechanical geniuses before we were to see any really usable contrivances that would allow the logging industry to make use of anything that looks like what we know today as a chain saw.

STIHL

Many factors contributed to producing the modern chain saw. But without doubt, the credit for developing the world's first workable chain saw must be given to Andreas Stihl. By 1923, this young German inventor had already invented a gasoline-powered washing machine. As is the case with all inventive geniuses, Andreas Stihl was endowed with a great natural curiosity and the inquisitiveness to ask why a certain function could not be improved upon.

When he observed the laborings of loggers in the forests that surrounded his home, he naturally questioned the slow and tedious efforts he witnessed and wondered why he could not adapt his gasoline-powered washing machine principle to a form of lumbering. With this goal in sight, he began to produce what eventually became the world's first practical chain saw. Surprisingly it looked very much like the machines we use today.

A great deal of refinement was needed to progress from Stihl's first ideas to a machine that would be truly practical in the forests. See Figs. 1-1 through 1-6. Stihl was aware of the progress being made in America by Charles Ferguson who had developed a gasoline-powered generator. Knowing of this source of power, Stihl's first attempt at a workable chain saw was designed to be powered by a generator. It was actually an electric chain saw. Ferguson's generator turned out to be the foundation for what we know today as the Homelite Company, one of the world's leading chain saw manufacturers.

In 1926, three years after he developed his electric chain saw, Stihl produced a chain saw that did indeed effectively cut logs.

Fig. 1-1. The first Stihl chain saw produced in 1929 (courtesy of Stihl Inc.).

However, its practicality was limited because it was so heavy. The motor actually had to be removed from the cutting attachment to move the contraption and then reattached to operate it.

Even with all these deficiencies, the chain saw was now a workable unit and phase II was nearing its end. All that remained was for engineering to develop a smaller, more efficient portable gasoline-powered motor. History provided the impetus.

With the ushering in of the 1930s and World War II, engineers world-wide provided the necessary innovations to develop a usable power pack that would eventually make the chain saw practical. There were many refinements to Stihl's original designs, and by many persons. Stihl himself held over 400 international patents and 200 registered designs when he died in 1973. There were many other contributors to the process as well, but it was in Germany that the necessary ingredients were present to produce the most refinements.

As Germany prepared to wage war, many of the loggers found their way into the factories where wages were higher and work easier than in the forests. This left Germany's logging industry decimated by a lack of laborers and provided the impetus for chain saw development to progress at a faster pace than in the rest of the world. By the time the war began, Germany had the only really efficient chain saw ready for use.

The story is often related how Allied troops on the move toward the German heartland were confronted more than once with paths blocked by trees felled across the roads. Knowing they were hot on the heels of the retreating troops, there was dismay at how the Germans could cut so many trees so quickly. It was not until after the war that we found this feat was attributable to the advanced German chain saw design.

After the war, many manufacturers began to produce good chain saws. Our own Seabees had used the Disston saws with

14

Mercury motors from 1942 on and I recall selling a one-man Disston as early as 1953. Homelite and McCulloch got into the act around 1948. I. E. L., a forerunner of Pioneer, was developing chain saws around that time and the Mall Tool Company was licensed to use some of the Stihl designs in the late 1930s and early 1940s. With the end of phase II of the chain saw evolutionary story, all that remained to get the industry really off the ground was a very innovative gentleman named Joe Cox, a bag lunch and a couple of timber beetles! Here comes phase III!

All the time Andreas Stihl and everyone else were involved in developing chain saws, the one thing that escaped their genius was a really practical cutting chain. In the evolutionary process, everyone assumed the end result had to be the mechanization of existing modes of wood cutting saws: the crosscut saw, band saws, hand saws, and circular saws. Each design or refinement of existing designs was directed toward this end. The chains that were produced were heavy, awkward contrivances based on the only ideas available to the wood industry in those early days. Extreme patience, experience and a lot of time was required to sharpen and repair such chains. Very few loggers could handle it.

OREGON CHAIN

Joe Cox was one of those working with these tools who questioned their practicality and he was constantly trying to envision a better chain. As the story goes, Joe was on his lunch break one day while straddling a large log that had recently been felled. As he sat there in the still of the forest, he heard the ever-present timber beetles gnawing wood just under the bark of the log. Lifting a section of the bark from the tree, Joe became enthralled at what he was watching. The beetles were equipped with cutting mandibles that enabled them to gnaw through the spruce logs with amazing speed. Looking closer, he noticed that the secret to their efficiency was that each mandible had a built-in guide which determined that the mandibles cut wood of just the right thickness to allow the beetles to work practically effortlessly!

Basing the design of a cutting chain on the creations of nature as exemplified in the timber beetle, Joe Cox was able to develop what was known in 1947 as the Cox chain. This chain used alternating cutters with rakers. It is the chipper chain as we know it today. Working in his basement, Joe Cox and a helper manufactured and sold more than $300,000 worth of chain in 1947, his first year of operation, and then sold his patent rights to a marketing

Fig. 1-2. A Disston model D-100 chain saw. Built in 1942 by the Mercury Motors Division for the Henry Disston Co., this saw utilized a scratcher type of chain that rode on the outside of the bar rather than in a groove as modern saws do. In order to engage the clutching mechanism, the rear handle must be depressed. This is unlike modern saws that utilize an automatically engaging centrifugal clutch.

16

Fig. 1-3. The Homelite model 20 MCS chain saw. This was the first production model of Homelite saws, manufactured in 1948. It weighed 48 pounds. Holes were stamped into the bar to reduce some weight. The chain was of the float type which required swivelling of the rear handle assembly in order to maintain the carburetor in an upright position when cutting horizontally.

Fig. 1-4. The Sten saw was manufactured and marketed by the Sten Co. of New York City in 1947. This Rube Goldberg contraption used a 4-cycle motor. Through a series of gears, cams, chains and cranks, it drove (or attempted to drive) a 5-foot cross-cut saw blade at a rate of about 600 strokes a minute. While the blade was oscillating, the operator was expected to lower it into the log by means of the handle just to the top of the blade. The whole device could be tilted to a horizontal position in order to cut trees down. Even the owners' manual recommended using an axe on small trees!

Fig. 1-5. I am attempting to operate a mechanical bow saw developed in the 1920s. The band saw blade rotated around two large pulleys by use of a hand crank. It was an innovation of the hand-powered saws developed in those years before powered saws became a reality.

19

Fig. 1-6. A "precision" chain saw manufactured in Danbury, CT and Montreal, Canada, about 1939. The scratcher chain was tensioned by an intricate bowing out of a spring within the upper housing upon which the chain also ran.

entrepreneur named John Gray. Mr. Gray was responsible for transforming Joe Cox's chipper chain into the worldwide standard that it is today, called Oregon Chain, a division of Omark Industries of Portland, Oregon.

With the development of a practical chain, phase III was concluded. The Oregon chain is very practical, not only because of its remarkable cutting efficiency, but more so because anyone can quickly learn to sharpen it with consistency. From that point on, it has simply been a matter of developing better chain saws of lighter weight, faster cutting capability and of greater durability. There is no end in sight.

Inventors like Andreas Stihl, Charles Ferguson, and Joe Cox had the foresight and the ingenuity to give us the tool we call the chain saw. Where we go from here is anybody's guess. The possibilities for future development are limitless. Perhaps you will come up with an innovation which will totally reshape the entire chain saw industry!

TYPICAL BREAKDOWN OF A CHAIN SAW

Figure 1-7 shows a typical chain saw broken down in a very simplified manner so as to make it more understandable for the occasional user. Many insignificant small parts such as screws, nuts, bolts, gaskets and washers have been eliminated for the sake of simplicity. However, everything of importance has been left in and the reader should be able to recognize all the parts as they relate to his saw.

The saw I have chosen in this breakdown is an Echo 500VL and the construction is typical of most foreign saws and only slightly different from some domestic saws. The main difference to be found will be in the split crankcase as opposed to the one-piece crankcase found in most domestic saws. Another difference will be in the plastic gas tank and oil reservoir enclosed within housings as opposed to saws that have tanks as part of the castings.

This should provide a fairly good guide to the location of the starter systems, the flywheel and ignition parts, the crankshaft and the power head, and (from left to right) the clutch and sprocket. If you refer to my simplified descriptions of a chain in Chapter 6, you will see that all of this is enclosed within housings and includes a fuel system, handles, motor mounts, etc. The bar and chain movement is the resulting visible action of everything that makes up the saw.

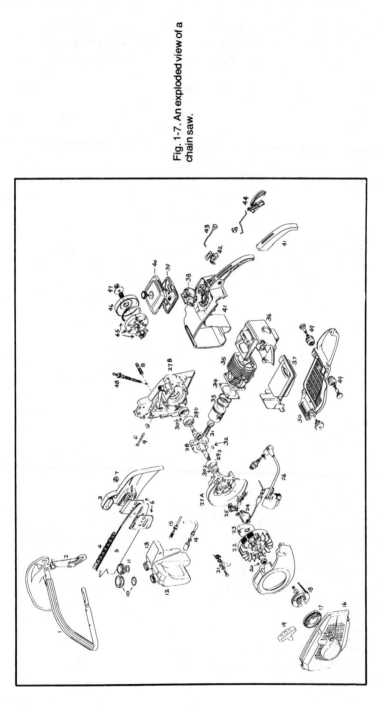

Fig. 1-7. An exploded view of a chain saw.

During the course of repairing your saw, you should refer to this breakdown frequently as I describe each specific repair and as I guide you through the complete care of your chain saw.

The average chain saw, regardless of brand or model, will consist of approximately 463 parts. That's counting all the screws, washers, bolts, nuts, gaskets and seals, as well as some gadgets and whatzits that you'll come across. To try to ennumerate each and every part on a diagram like Fig. 1-7 would be confusing and boring as well.

What I have shown here are the important parts for you to examine. You'll just have to understand that each housing is held in place with screws, each of which will have a washer with it, that there will be gaskets wherever castings are joined together and that there will be some 400 assorted small parts that I have not shown. As you disassemble your saw, remember to make a mental note of these parts as you go along. Generally, what I have pictured will give you a condensed version of a chain saw from tip to end. The following is a listing of the important components of a chain saw.

1. Front or top handle bar
2. Front handle bar brace
3. Sprocket cover, sometimes called a clutch cover
4. Chain
5. Guide bar
6. Bar plates
7. Bar stud nuts
8. Bar studs
9. Tensioning screw and pin
10. Gas cap and gasket
11. Oil reservoir cap and gasket
12. Gas tank
13. Oil reservoir
14. Gas line with fuel pickup; direct line to carburetor
15. Oil line with pickup
16. Starter housing
17. Starter spring; recessed inside starter housing
18. Starter rotor with rope
19. Starter handle
20. Flywheel nut
21. Starter pawl assembly
22. Flywheel
23. Breaker box cover

24. Condenser

25. Breaker points

26. Coil, with high tension lead, spark plug terminal and boot and spark plug

27A. Left side crankcase half

27B. Right side crankcase half

28. Crankshaft

29A. Crankshaft main ball bearing, left side or magneto side

29B. Crankshaft main ball bearing, right side or power side

30A. Crankshaft seal, magneto side

30B. Crankshaft seal, power side

31. Connecting rod

32. Flywheel key

33. Piston with piston rings

34. Cylinder head gasket

35. Cylinder head

36. Cylinder shroud

37. Muffler; sometimes found to the right side of cylinder

38. Carburetor, will have a gasket between it and housing

39. Air filter

40. Air filter cover

41. Air box assembly; sometimes called rear handle assembly

42. Switch; on-off

43. Choke rod and button

44. Trigger assembly and throttle rod

45. Clutch assembly; consists of spider, clutch shoes and clutch spring

46. Sprocket and clutch drum assembly

47. Sprocket bearing, washer and nut

48. Automatic oiling pump assembly

49. Antivibration buffers. Front handle brace and bar as well as the rear handle assembly will be isolated from the motor assembly through use of these buffers

50. Bottom handle brace

Chapter 2
Selecting a Chain Saw

When I started in the chain saw business in 1952, there were only two chain saws of any distinct quality available: Homelite and McCulloch. Othere saws then available have long since been relegated to the scrap heap or to the antique collections found in some dealers' showrooms.

Among those now defunct brands were Disston, Strunk, Mall, Porter-Cable, Mono and Lancaster. Pioneer and Lombard are still with us, to a limited degree, and Homelite and McCulloch are among the most widely sold saws in the industry. Today, the potential purchaser of a chain saw has dozens of quality saws to choose from—both in models and in brands.

FOREIGN VERSUS DOMESTIC SAWS

In 1952, there was hardly a foreign saw to be found in America. Stihl was by far the leader in the industry. But back then you could only find Stihl saws in Europe, the Northwest and especially in British Columbia. By comparison today, those seeking quality in a chain saw will think of the foreign products first—those manufactured in Germany, Sweden or Japan. They have gained a very firm foothold in the chain saw field today. The foreign products have led the industry in such important engineering features as vibration dampening, quiet mufflers, chrome impregnation of the cylinders, safety features, and in overall durability of design.

There is really no valid justification for America lagging behind the foreign competition in chain saws. After all, it was

America who forged to the forefront in the Industrial Revolution. Why then the slide to second place? If I were to expound my philosophies on the subject here, the covers of this book would not be wide enough to hold them. We simply must recognize that it has happened. Domestic manufacturers are making renewed efforts to get back into the professional quality market after going through an era when they directed all their attention to the occasional user market because of the tremendous profits to be made there.

In considering this question of foreign versus domestic competition, I must relate an incident that vividly points out the situation. It happened in 1972 at a distributor show. We were being shown the new models of saws, lawnmowers, snowblowers, snowmobiles and brush saws for the coming year. We were also being subjected to the usual rhetoric designed to buoy our enthusiasm and fill order forms.

The subject of one meeting centered on snowmobiles; those products of man's cunning intended to make us believe that when days are cold and the countryside is covered with snow the *only* way to enjoy nature's bountiful beauty of winter was to climb aboard these mechanical monsters. All we had to do was seat ourselves behind a 20-horsepower motor, switch it to life and roar across the serene countryside at full bore wafting our hazy blue exhaust into the crackling winter air. Of course this joyful ride occurs while emitting ear-splitting reverberations throughout the forests at a decibel level intended to let every living creature know that we are kings of all we survey.

The point the eloquent speaker was trying to make at the time was that there was a very sinister force loose around us—those advocates of peace and quiet, those preachers of change—who, if they were not quelled, would press for the regulation of noise levels in our most precious economy! We were being told that if we did not band together to repulse these faddists they just might attain some governmental regulation of noise levels in these mighty machines! And, we were told, such regulation would mean the demise of our snowmobile business because who in their right mind would want to buy such a machine if they could not roar it to life and enjoy the sense of power riding such a machine gives them!

The argument being presented, in addition to this creed, was that it was impossible to construct a muffler that could effectively dampen the noise levels of such motors. Now I'm not an engineer, but all the while this was going on I was sitting there looking at a foreign brushcutter with a tiny 2-horsepower motor that had a muffler on it almost the size of the motor. When it was run just a half-hour earlier, you could have made a phone call right next to it and heard every word being spoken to you. The noise level had been so effectively dampened that it was a pleasure to use the tool. I couldn't for the life of me grasp the reasons why one foreign manufacturer could totally dampen sound while a domestic company felt it was impossible to do so.

Of course we have now come to decibel regulation. And we have found that it is possible to build effective muffling systems. But it only occurred after we were forced into it and only after the foreign manufacturers showed us that it was possible!

America's slide to second place in the chain saw industry occurred most visibly after the energy crisis of 1973. Until then, most professional loggers were using either Homelite or McCulloch chain saws exclusively. When the market expanded (exploded) into a consumer oriented field, it is my contention that the domestic producers went full bore into that market. They ignored the needs of the professional and sought the profits to be gained in the consumer related area.

At that point, the professionals began to turn to the foreign saws for their product. From that day on there has been no turning back. The foreign saws had a foot in the door, and try as they might, Homelite and McCulloch have been unable to dislodge them. Today, the largest part of the Homelite and McCulloch production is found in discount style outlets while the quality foreign saws have been able to maintain a firm foothold in the professional trade. The balance continues to tip more and more in that direction as additional quality foreign saws find their way into the American marketplace each year.

The only domestic producer that is successfully attempting to keep pace with the foreign manufacturers is Poulan. Over the past five years they have produced the only domestic saws with silicone-aluminum cylinders, vibration systems and quiet-tone mufflers. While some of their models still utilize the plated cylinders, they are at least attempting to improve their standing. In value, they are ahead of their American competition.

FITTING THE SAW TO THE USER'S NEEDS

I recommend that you buy a foreign saw. But which one do you select from the hundreds of models that are available? Try to fit a saw to your needs. To do so, you must first define those needs.

Because this book is primarily designed for the occasional user or the small wood producer, I will try to assess those needs. Such a user is most likely to be cutting wood to supply a wood stove that is serving as a supplement or a replacement for an energy devouring heating plant. In this capacity, those needs can safely be put at somewhere between 1 and 10 cords per year. One to 5 cords will be enough to simply supplement a heating system. From 5 to 10 cords will be enough for you to rely entirely on wood heat.

Two factors come into play in sensibly selecting a chain saw to fill these needs. One factor is the size, in diameter, of the trees or logs to be tackled. The other factor is the size of the expenditure you are willing to make.

Let's first consider the person who wants to simply supplement a heating system. More than likely, the wood will be purchased in 4-foot lengths and delivered to the home. Almost without exception, the diameter of such logs will be no larger than 14 inches. This is the most efficient sized trees for a small producer to cut, load and deliver. It stands to reason that this purchaser can satisfy those needs with a 14-inch chain saw.

On the other hand, if a person expects to cut more than five cords of wood a year, and it might be in the 16-inch diameter size, it stands to reason that this person will be best off with a saw that utilizes a 16-inch guide bar. The dividing line between a lightweight saw and a medium saw is 5 cords of wood.

Now let's put together some basics about what is a lightweight 14-inch saw and a medium weight 16-inch saw. Let's also straighten out the confusion about cubic-inch displacement and horsepower. For all practical purposes, you can assume that each cubic inch of displacement is equal to 1 horsepower.

Because we are in the process of converting to the metric system in America and because most foreign saws will be rated in cubic centimeters, you must also avoid the confusion concerning cubic centimeters. A foreign product that is rated at 48 cubic centimeters is a 3.0-cubic-inch motor (or a 3-horsepower saw).

Lightweight saws are those rated from 1.6hp to 2.3hp. Medium-weight saws are rated from 2.5hp to 3.7hp. Lightweight saws will have bar lengths of from 10 to 14 inches while the medium-weight saws will utilize bar lengths of 16, 20, and 24 inches. Beyond the medium-weight saws, there are professional saws with horsepower ratings up to 6.0 cubic inches and bar lengths exceeding 24 inches. I do not intend to get into a discussion of the merits and needs of these larger saws. The intention of this book is to inform the new, occasional user of saws. You need me, but the professional doesn't!

SEEKING ADVICE ON SAW SELECTION

So what saw does the occasional user need to buy? Well, there are several routes to go. First, you can seek out the advice of professional users, tree surgeons, loggers and wood producers. In following this course of action you must keep in mind one fact. If you were to ask 50 different professional cutters, using 50 different saws, you can safely expect 50 different answers! But the most important thing to remember is that if the truth were known, professional users are loyal to certain brands for only one reason. They are most likely getting the best deal from a dealer carrying that particular brand.

Professionals are very dollar conscious. They also drive the hardest bargains and they demand outrageous service. These are facts. And in saying so, perhaps I will alienate many professionals. But I intend to tell it as it is in this book. If you seek out municipal departments to find out what saws they use, look deeper! Most municipalities buy their saws on bid. They are forced to accept what their purchasing agents deem the best dollar figure. Many times this is with complete disregard for dollar value or quality.

The lowest bidder always gets the business in municipal affairs. If this is not the case, then there is often collusion between certain dealers and local agencies for the purchase of materials, including chain saws. Don't look to the professionals or municipalities for advice; it is almost always useless.

Another source of advice you can seek is consumer publications. Again, I am going to alienate some readers here! I have spent 27 years in the chain saw business and I know the business! I can safely say that consumer publications are wrong more times than not when they make recommendations concerning chain saws. Surely they make specification comparisons, but they usually cannot go beyond what the manufacturers supply in written information.

For example, I have seen examples where they have recommended a Remington chain saw as being a good quality item, and, in the same analysis, put down a John Deere saw as being inferior. The fact of the matter is that they were both the same saw because at that time Remington was building the John Deere saw! At other times, I have seen Sears Roebuck chain saws recommended highly, with complete disregard for the fact that the saw being recommended was built by the Roper Company, and—unknown to the potential customer—nobody but Sears can supply certain component parts for that particular saw.

The Roper Company is under contract to supply only Sears with parts for their saws and no other saw dealer in the country can buy certain components to repair that saw. Even the Federal Trade Commission has been incapable of overturning that arrangement.

Therefore, I contend that consumer publications are inadequate. They are simply unable to properly advise you. To whom does one turn to gain the necessary facts of chain saw comparisons? The most reliable information can be obtained from chain saw servicing dealers.

Try to pick out the dealer in your area who does the most servicing of chain saws. Pick out a dealer who services all brands of saws if possible. Pick out a dealer who carries several brands of saws, the more the better. Find out how long he has been in business and how long he has carried the different brands. Ask to see his repair quarters to see which brands are in for repair most frequently. This is not always a true assessment because there might be only certain brands in use in certain areas. However, it is a good starting point.

Ask the dealer's assessment of the different brands of saws he carries. Notice if he is overstocked in certain brands and if he is pushing you into a certain brand because of this. Beware of the dealer who is too pushy. You should be allowed to make up your own mind in your own time. Choose a dealer who lets you try a saw right there at his shop. Just running it is not enough; you should actually make some trial cuts in wood while you are there. Make sure he will set up the saw, service it before you leave, tune it and take care of everything necessary before you buy.

Ask about the availability of parts for the different brands. Most of all, do business with a dealer who is busy. Ask around to inquire about the reputation of the dealer with whom you are contemplating doing business. Does he honor warranties? Does he stand behind his product? Does he pay his bills? Just be sure he is a reputable businessman. After that, look up other dealers. Compare notes to see if you are getting factual answers.

I would caution a purchaser about one thing more. Don't try to beat the dealer down in price. If he recognizes he is going to have to take a loss of profit to a customer, this will cause him to be insincere in his approach. It is much better to pay a fair price for a product and let the dealer know you expect him to provide adequate service for the dollars you are paying him.

I find that those customers who are always seeking something off the top are the ones I'd rather not see back again. On the other hand, if I have made a fair profit and have had a sincere relationship with a customer, that person is always welcomed when the slightest problem arises and I'm anxious to take care of those needs. The person who beats me out of a buck is the one I'd rather not see again. Another concern is that if a dealer is willing to discount a product, there might be something wrong with it or perhaps he is panicking and feels the need to move it out. So beware of discounted prices.

LIGHTWEIGHT SAWS

Now I want to get down to specifics in recommending some saws. For the user who is cutting about 2 or 3 cords of wood a year, using a saw for household pruning, thinning underbrush, or cutting logs no larger than 10 inches in diameter, I recommend a lightweight saw in the 2hp to 2.3hp category. The choices here are the Poulan Micro 25 line or the Poulan Super 25 series saws.

Poulan

The Micro 25 series comes in 10-inch, 12-inch and 14-inch bar lengths. They all utilize the same 2.0hp motor with identical automatic oiling systems. While these saws are the bottom of the Poulan line, they are remarkably dependable. One of the features I particularly like is the location of the carburetor. It is tucked into a box separate from the rest of the saw. It resists the tendency to become caked with dirt and residue because it is not in the way of the cooling air flow. While it is true that you need to remove the carburetor air box cover to adjust the carburetor, this is not a serious concern. I'd rather have it so as long as I can be certain it is not going to become packed with dirt during use.

As you go up in the Micro series to the 12-inch and 14-inch bars, you will notice that the top handle is covered with a plastic covering on the 12-inch saw and a foam rubber grip on the 14-inch saw. The 12-inch and 14-inch bars will come equipped with sprocket noses and the chains will be chromed. This is not the case with the 10-inch bar and chain. It is important to get chromed chains because their life between sharpenings is far extended over the nonchromed ones. Other than these differences, there are no mechanical advantages from the 10-inch to the 14-inch Poulan Micro 25 saw series.

Stepping up to the Super 25 series, you will again find no marked differences in the mechanical construction of the saws. The Super 25 DA and the Super 25 CVA will have only one basic difference. That is the vibration isolation features of the CVA saw plus a padded top handle. Both saws utilize a 2.3hp motor and identical oiling systems. Both saws have combination manual and automatic oiling systems. But don't be fooled here! These are *not* separate systems. If one system fails, the other system will not work independently of it. Therefore you are not really getting a true backup system. The automatic system works through the same pump and orifices as the manual. If it fails, the manual system also fails and vice versa.

The Micro 25 series of saws is totally adequate for the user who anticipates using up to 3 cords of wood a year. The Super 25 series saws in the Poulan line are capable of cutting up to 10 cords a year. I know of many professional users making very good use of the Super 25 series saws in their everyday work. If you intend to cut more than 5 cords of wood per year you should look into medium-weight saws rather than attempting to work a small lightweight saw too severely. I'm referring to making the most advantageous use of whatever saw you purchase. It only stands to reason that a small lightweight saw will be extended to its limits if you attempt to overwork it. Doing the same work, a medium-weight saw will have some reserve left to continue in years to come.

Homelite

Other lightweight saws available include the Homelites. You can choose from the XL, a 10-inch saw with 1.6hp motor, automatic oiling only, with a nonchromed chain and solid (nonsprocket nose) bar; the XL-2, a 12-inch saw utilizing sprocket nose bar, chromed chain, and a 1.6hp motor; and, the super 2, 2 14-inch saw, chromed chain, sprocket nose bar, and a 1.9hp motor.

While the Homelites in the lightweight series are not bad saws, I don't prefer them for several reasons. First, and most important, is the difficulty in repairing them. Unlike the Poulans, the carburetors are located where the cooling air flow goes right over them. This results in the carburetors becoming packed with dirt with any amount of usage. Another disadvantage I find is the single needle adjustment of the carburetor. Where two-needle carburetors have both high and low speed adjustments available, a single-needle carburetor is forced to make a concession because both low and high speed adjustments are made through the same needle.

The location of the carburetor inside the motor housing also makes it far more tedious to repair. The starter housing, bar and chain, spark plug, and motor housing all must be removed to get to the carburetor. Compared to the Poulans, the effort and time involved seems to be 10 times more.

The Homelite saws also have an added disadvantage in that the oil pickup line inside the oil reservoir is so designed that it occasionally causes oil to be forced into the motor rather than onto the bar and chain. This causes what is known as a *hydraulic lock* and this happens when the oil reservoir is filled to absolute capacity or when the saw is stored in such a position that the oil leaks into the cylinder head. Repairing a hydraulic lock is not very involved, but is typical with the Homelite lightweights and not so typical with some other saws.

Notice that the horsepower ratings of these saws are less than the Poulans and other saws I will mention further along. Even though they perform well, I prefer to have more horsepower if it is available at the same price or near the same price.

McCulloch

Another widely advertised saw is the McCulloch. These saws utilize 2.3hp motors and come in 10-inch, 12-inch, 14-inch and 16-inch bar lengths. They have automatic and manual oiling systems that are somewhat independent of each other. Again, as with the Homelites and Poulans, the 10-inch saws do not have sprocket nose bars and chromed chains, but the longer bar lengths will.

I cannot recommend the McCullochs very highly because I find them to be less than durable in many cases. Screws have a tendency to back out and their 310, 320, 330, and 340 series have a very complicated throttling control cable system that is costly to repair and cannot withstand heavy duty use.

The one feature about the small McCullochs that I disagree with is the self-sharpening chain that comes with them. These are chains designed to be sharpened by the user while the saw is running by causing a grinding stone to come in contact with the chain as it revolves around the sprocket of the saw. While the system works fairly well for the first few sharpenings, in continued usage the stone becomes worn as well as the chain, bar and sprocket. When these variables are all put together, it becomes almost impossible for the system to work effectively.

Because the occasional or novice user is not aware of the inadequacies of the sharpening system, he many times continues to use the saw when the chain is very dull. The resulting abuse of the bar and the rest of the saw can necessitate replacement of the bar. In my shop, we replace more McCulloch bars because of this kind of abuse than any other brand. I am opposed to the self-sharpening style of chain and defy anyone to find a "professional" cutter who will use it. There are many more reasons for my opposition explained in Chapter 7. To sum up my recommendations on the McCulloch saws, I would have to say that you could do better if you are looking for durability and soundness of design.

Stihl

Being the originator of chain saws, Stihl has continued to be well-accepted and a very well-designed saw line. Their small saws are no exception to this rule. Their current small saw, the 010 series, is a 2.3hp saw with a 14-inch or 16-inch bar, automatic oiling, very responsive vibration systems, extremely quiet mufflers, and separate compartments for the carburetors. There are both high-speed and low-speed needles for setting the motor rpm's, and the carburetor is out of the way of the air flow so it does not get dirty in use. Where the Homelites and McCullochs offer electronic ignitions, the Stihl utilizes a standard point and condensor set-up, much like the Poulan Micro series and it is an easy ignition to service. I like the 010 Stihl and I believe it is comparable to the Poulan in performance, durability and price.

Stihl also builds two other small saws: the 015 and the 020. Both of these saws can be purchased with 14-inch or 16-inch bars, sprocket nose, automatic oiling only, vibration isolated or solid. While they are both 1.93hp saws, the 020 is a professional model and sells for too much money for the occasional user to consider unless he feels he needs to spend that sum. The 015 saw is going to be phased out and I would suggest that the better buy for anyone would be the newly-designed 010 series for the added horsepower and the features mentioned above.

Echo

Another very well-designed saw to consider is the Echo line, imported from Japan. It comes in several models; the 302, which is a 1.6hp saw with a 12-inch bar, the 315, which is available in

12-inch and 14-inch bars, and the 351VL (standing for vibration-less), available in 14-inch and 16-inch sizes. A nice feature of the Echo line is the mahle-chrome cylinder design. Together with the Stihl, they are the only small saws utilizing this superior motor design.

The next Echo small saw, the 315, is a 1.8hp saw. The Echo 351 is a 2.3hp saw. They have only the automatic oiling system and they have a good muffling system. While very well engineered, they are a little difficult to work on and I find them just a little underpowered. You have to baby them a little. But owners of Echo saws can expect many years of service from the units if they are taken care of properly. They have standard ignitions very similar to the ignitions in those saws mentioned earlier and the ignitions are inexpensive to replace.

Skil

Other saws deserving mention here are the Skil saws. They seem to be finding their way into the market more lately and many are being sold in hardware stores and catalog showrooms. They are 2.3-horsepower saws with bars available in 12-inches, 14 inches and 16 inches. They usually have only manual oiling and the oiling systems are somewhat undependable and poorly constructed. While the carburetors are in separate enclosures, there is the typical problem of becoming blocked with dirt inside the carburetor inlet.

I also find them a little noisy and they seem to vibrate excessively. The mufflers have a habit of loosening because there is only one screw holding the entire muffler in place. Another problem area I often find is the ignition cover which has a poorly designed method of being secured. As a result, the point box, which it is suppose to seal, often becomes dirty and causes an ignition malfunction. I rate this saw somewhere below the others I have mentioned.

Another small saw sold in many areas is the Danarm. This is a saw made by Frontier Mfg. of Canada. Its major claim to fame is that it is made for many other companies and is "branded" under several labels. For example, the Jonsereds 361, the Partner "Lil Partner," and the Husqvarna "Husky" are *not* made by those very fine manufacturers. They are all Frontier saws branded for the various companies.

The problems I find with these saws are almost exactly those encountered with the Skil line. This includes blockages of the carburetor inlets, excessive vibration, poor oiling systems, insecure mufflers, being noisy and being undependable. I would caution anyone against purchasing "branded" saws. Manufacturers back-up procedures are limited at best and parts supply can be a problem.

The saws mentioned above are all capable of serving an owner who intends to cut up to 5 cords of wood a year. Some will serve you better than others. Rather than making recommendations in favor of one or another brand or model, I have gone the other route. I have pointed out the problem areas as I have encountered them over the past years. This is surely a different approach to what will be found in the various consumer digests and I believe it will better serve to guide the reader in choosing a lightweight saw.

MEDIUM-WEIGHT SAWS

The person who is cutting more than 5 cords but less than 10 cords has the widest possible choice of high quality saws. My favorite saws are the Jonsereds. Jonsereds are constructed in such a way that when a housing part is broken you will need to replace only that one piece—not a complicated and involved housing. For instance, the rear handle on all Jonsereds is just that—a rear handle. Two screws remove it from the main housing and nothing more is required. This kind of single-piece design is utilized throughout the entire line and contributes to economical repair when needed.

Jonsereds

Another feature of the Jonsereds line that I like is the vertical engine. This feature makes it simple to work on the motor, the mufflers, vibration systems, housings, handles, and all other parts as well. Comparing this to the Homelite or McCulloch line, you will find that if one rear handle breaks the component required to make the repair involves replacing the entire carburetor housing and even the entire gas tank in some models of McCullochs. This kind of repair will cost a Homelite or McCulloch owner in excess of $35. A rear handle repair on a Jonsereds will run less than $15.

Jonsereds saws utilize mahle-chrome cylinders that are far longer lasting. This kind of engineering insures that the saws actually increase in performance over the first several hours of life. On the other hand, the performance of plated cylinders is downhill from day one. The mdeium-weight Jonsereds start with the model 510SP, a 16-inch, 3.0hp saw; followed by the 451E, at 15 inches and 2.7hp; and the 49SP, 15-inch or 18-inch with 3.0hp. I use the

49SP and find it most comfortable for me. The vibration dampening systems are among the most responsive in the industry.

Echo

Another fine line of medium-weight saws is the Echo brand from Japan. I can recall when we poked fun at the Japanese manufacturers because we thought their products were cheaply constructed or simply copies. Well it's different today! If you look around, you must admit there is hardly a quality camera, binocular, radio or television that is not manufactured in Japan. The same quality is being put into their chain saws and the prices at the moment are very attractive.

While a little heavy for the motor size of the Echo, this is really a reflection of the quality of design. The Echo line starts with the 452VL, a 16-inch saw with a 2.7hp motor. Following this is the 500VL, 16-inch or 20-inch with a 3.04hp motor and the 60 CS, a 3.6hp saw with 16-inch or 20-inch bar. Then there is the 602VL which has a 3.6 hp motor and will also handle 16-inch or 20-inch bars.

All Echos, with the exception of the 60CS, have excellent vibration dampening systems and most will have adjustable automatic oilers with manual overrides. All models except the 60CS have horizontal motors, mahle-chromed cylinders, chain grabbers and hand guards. The muffling systems on the Echos are also very effective. All the handles are covered with rubber for comfort and safety.

While I find the engineering of Echo to be excellent, they are somewhat difficult to repair. This is due to the horizontal motor system which causes components to be difficult to reach. However, they are easily as durable a product as I have come across.

Stihl

The originator of the chain saw was Stihl. There has been a legendary acceptance of German engineering as being the world's finest. Excellence has certainly been true of their chain saws. Mahle-chromed cylinders, quiet mufflers, choice of vibration dampening or not in many models, cushioned grips, safety features, and other qualities all make Stihl one of the world's finest saws.

Stihl medium-weight saws start with the 028 series in what is called the AV (anti-vibration) or Wood Boss. Utilizing a 2.7hp motor, the 028 is a vertical engine saw and will handle 15-inch or

18-inch bars. The next step is the 031 AV; it has a 2.93hp motor and 16-inch or 20-inch bars. A new 032 AV model has recently appeared. It has a 3.4 hp saw and it will also handle 16-inch or 20-inch bars. It utilizes a 45-degree motor. While it performs beautifully, it is a little difficut to work on. In addition to these saws, Stihl makes an 041 AV, a 3.7hp saw and the 041 FB of the same horsepower. Both are capable of handling up to 20-inch bars. The FB does not have the antivibration systems and it is a little noisier.

If there is any criticism I might have of the Stihl line, it would have to be with questioning the wisdom of their electronic ignition systems. While in theory they should perform better than conventional ignitions, and supposedly last longer, I would caution the purchaser about the potential cost of replacement parts should the system fail. They can be more costly to replace than conventional systems and also more costly than competitive electronic systems found in almost every other brand.

The big advantage of an electronic system is that the spark is designed to advance as the rpm's of the saw are increased (thereby providing more top-end power). Another feature is that condensation should not have as much of a detrimental effect on the ignition as with conventional points. My current preference is to stick with conventional systems. The occasional user is looking 10 years down the road under normal usage before needing to replace points and condensors in a standard ignition.

I mentioned earlier that Poulan has made the most determined effort to keep abreast of the competition from foreign manufacturers and I must make one recommendation here in that respect. A newer model in their line is the Poulan 3400. It is destined to claim a fair share of the market in the next few years. It is a 3.4-cubic-inch displacement engine, it will carry a 16-inch or 20-inch bar, it has excellent vibration systems and it has cushioned handles. It also utilizes electronic ignition and has independent manual and automatic oiling systems. The cylinder is silicone-aluminum and the saw has a very quiet muffling system. This saw turns up very fast and it is a most impressive unit.

Other saws that deserve mention in this chapter are two Swedish imports: Husqvarna and Partner. They are among the most dependable and fastest cutting saws available. Many times when we compete in cutting contests with other chain saw users and dealers, we find ourselves up against many users with Huskies and Partners and they always perform very well.

In the lightweight categories, Husqvarna model 34 series are not constructed by Husqvarna. They are either Frontier or Skil chain saws. Therefore, I would discount them immediately from my recommendations. Husqvarna does manufacture two other series of saws worthy of mention here. One is the 44 series. These saws come with or without chain brakes. The models 44 and 44CB are identical except for the braking feature. They have 44 cubic centimeters of displacement so they can be considered a 2.3hp saw. Both have vibration isolation, automatic oiling, electronic ignitions, and will accept 14-inch or 16-inch bars.

The Husqvarna 61 series is similar because it also features the chain brake on the 61CB and has the 61CC without chain brake. These saws have vibration isolation, electronic ignition, automatic oiling, and both have 61 cubic centimeters or about 3.8hp motors. A feature of the 61CB is the "automatic" chain brake that will activate itself in the event of kickback without the need for the operator's hand banging it to a stopped position. This is unlike any other chain brake offered on other saws and it certainly is a feature to be considered when buying a chain saw.

Partner only builds two saws for the casual user. The S50 and the S55 are both considered 3.4hp, utilize electronic ignitions and automatic oiling, and will accept 16-inch or 20-inch bars comfortably. The S55 has vibration isolation while the S50 is a solid saw.

While you will have a little difficulty locating Partner or Husqvarna dealers in many areas, both saws have to be considered among the finest engineered saws available. Breakdowns are minimal and performance is high. I would caution a potential purchaser to be assured of parts supply when buying either of these saws because I have experienced a little difficulty in getting parts in the past. However, this problem occurs with all manufacturers and dealers from time to time and usually for very legitimate reasons. These problems have a way of straightening out and everyone along the line makes a sincere effort to have the parts on hand because nobody makes money until a part is sold.

CYLINDER CONSTRUCTION

There are two methods of cylinder construction in use today in the chain saw industry: chrome plating and chrome impregnation. With the exception of a new, larger saw from Poulan, all American saws are constructed with a chrome plating system of the cylinder walls of the motor. In manufacturing, a coating of .0001 of an inch of chrome is applied to the cylinder walls. This allows the piston to move easily within the cylinder. It is extremely hard and it prevents the walls from wearing.

The foreign method, perfected by Stihl, is to impregnate the walls of the cylinder with chrome. In this manner, there is actually a heavier factor of chrome applied which, in theory, lasts longer. Which one does give longer life is academic because they both fail. I prefer the latter method for another reason. A chrome-impregnated motor requires a break-in period. Saw motors so constructed will actually perform about 10 percent better after the first several hours of running.

With plated cylinders the performance from day one cannot be improved upon. Of the saws mentioned thus far, Poulan, Homelite, and McCulloch utilize a chrome plating process while Stihl and Echo use the mahle-chrome system. To be absolutely accurate, the Poulan Micro series reverses the process and coats the piston instead of the cylinder walls to provide ease of movement.

CONSTRUCTION FEATURES

In considering the comparative merits of all saw brands, there are certain construction features you should keep in mind. First, I would look for safety bars and chains as a preference over chain brakes because they are *always* there to work for you. Chain brakes can become inoperable. I prefer a saw with vibration isolation features, chain grabbers and guarded handles for the operator's right hand. Safety throttles are a very fine additional feature. They prevent a saw from being activated accidentally and they assure that the operator's right hand is always in control of the saw. I would also look for a saw with a padded or rubber-covered top handle for comfort, safety and positive handling.

After all of this, I would compare the performance in actual cutting circumstances. The final concern will be price. I have intentionally avoided attempting to quote prices because six months from now any prices I might state will be obsolete. The industry is experiencing a price spiral comparable to all other commodities. Prices change regularly every six months or less. Until 1974, prices in the chain saw industry remained comparatively constant. With the chain saw taking its place as a desirable and necessary tool in our society, it has become subject to the same inflationary trends as clothes, cars, food and other necessities of life.

Any of the saws I have recommended are capable of being lifetime saws in the hands of a competent and careful owner. Ten cords of wood for these medium-weight saws is barely a workout—providing they are cared for. I would recommend any of them to anyone who has the need for such a product and is prepared to make the expenditure to buy one.

Try each and every one of them in several cuts to determine which saw balances best, which one has the weight factor desired, the noise level sought, and the appropriate safety factors. *Remember*—only buy a saw with which you can be assured of obtaining quick, efficient and economical service and repairs. Look for good servicing dealers. Beware of overstocks, closeouts and discount prices. Don't be pushed into buying. Buy only *after* test cutting with a saw. Don't buy a pig in a poke! Buy from reputable dealers only. Don't take the word of friends or other users without taking into consideration all the facts surrounding the reasons for such advice. Look for the most features for your money and be sure to buy a safe saw.

Now you are ready to go into the marketplace and buy a chain saw. After you've done that, come back to this book and read the next chapter. It has to do with setting up your saw and getting it ready to give you many long years of service.

Chapter 3
So You've
Bought a Chain Saw!

So you've bought a chain saw! Now you have it home and you can't wait to try it out. I hope you've followed my advice in the previous chapter and had the saw tuned and serviced at the dealer's showroom before making the purchase. Perhaps it is a gift or you have succumbed to impulse buying and acquired your saw from a nonservicing outlet or a catalog sales house. Whatever the case, I will give you some advice about your unit in this chapter.

You'd be amazed at the number of phone calls I get from my customers asking such simple questions as: What is the correct oil/gas ratio mix for my saw? How do I tension the chain? How do you clean the air filter? And so on.

Many of these questions are from people who have purchased their saw from me and had to put up with the 15 minute spiel I insist on going through with every saw I sell. In many instances, they've forgotten what I told them or else they didn't listen. Occasionally, they have lost their owners' manual or are borrowing a saw and need to know the particulars. In any case, there are certain basics you need to know to get the most satisfaction from your unit.

THE GAS/OIL MIX

Perhaps the most confusion or uncertainty you will have in readying your saw is the gas/oil mix. Most manufacturers recommend a certain mix—*if* you use their motor oil. Others will simply say: Use a good quality SAE 30 motor oil mixed in a certain way. It is very easy to get confused.

I recommend that you try to obtain an oil that is marketed by the manufacturer of the brand of saw you have purchased. This can still be confusing because, for instance, Homelite markets two different weight oils: one is 30-weight to be mixed 16:1 and the other is a 40-weight to be mixed 32:1. Some manufacturers do not have an oil carrying their name. McCulloch recommends a 40:1 mix and Stihl gives you a choice of from 16:1, 32:1, or 40:1—with the same oil! So what mix do you use?

Whatever you do, *never* use a regular motor oil—SAE 30. *Always* use a 2-cycle oil and preferably one that specifies use for chain saws. Never use what is referred to as "outboard motor oil" or "snowmobile oil" that is generally mixed 40:1 or 50:1. Outboard motors are water-cooled and reach and maintain a constant temperature. Snowmobiles are used when temperatures are at or below zero. This is entirely different from the conditions under which a chain saw is asked to perform.

Chain saws work all year round and sometimes when the temperatures are in the 90s. It is often used for work close to the ground where dirt will be a factor in lessening the air cooling efficiency. Chain saws are air-cooled and on a hot day they can reach extremely high temperatures. Oils must be capable of retaining their lubricating effectiveness under extreme conditions when used in these saws as compared with outboards or snowmobiles.

Even 2-cycle lawnmower oils are not asked to perform the function of chain saw oils because lawnmower engines have governors that prevent the motors from reaching the high revolutions at which chain saws turn. The oil that is to be used in a chain saw must be of the highest quality imaginable because more is demanded of it. Pick an oil that is recommended by the saw manufacturer. At least if the motor fails, it will not be considered your fault if you have followed the manufacturer's recommendations.

Even though there are different ratios suggested by all saw manufacturers, you can be safe if you use a 24:1 mix and use a 40-weight oil that has a non parafinic base. Parafinic base oils can congeal and this will prohibit adequate lubrication. Look at the contents of the can and discard it if it has a parafin base. A 24:1 ratio will be adequate for almost every saw when you are using a 40-weight oil. This ratio is one 8-ounce can of oil to a gallon and a half of gas. Also, never use high test gas. Always use regular, with lead, because the lead in the gas is a lubricant itself.

Mix the gas by putting the oil into a clean gas can first. Then, as the gas pump fills the can, the oil will be mixed into a complete suspension and ready for use. Always shake the can well before pouring it into your saw to be sure the mixture is in total suspension. In the event you don't use your saw for several months, get rid of your gas mixture in a proper manner. By then the gas will have evaporated to some extent and you will have a different mixture than when you first mixed it. A gas/oil mixture should never be older than a month for best results.

Now that you have mixed your gas and filled your gas tank, the next step is to provide lubrication for the chain. It is always far better to use a bar and chain oil than to attempt chain lubrication with regular oils or cheap crankcase drainings. The viscosity of regular oils is such that it cannot possibly hold to the chain at the tremendous speeds of modern saws. Together with the sharpness and tensioning of the chain, the correct lubrication of the chain is the most important part of maintaining your saw properly.

Be sure to use a good quality bar oil. You will find that in the long run it will save you money on bar and chain replacement because the chain will not wear as quickly and will remain safer over the years. I have found that there is not a great difference in quality among brands of bar and chain oil. They all provide a good degree of stickiness and lubricate the chain well. However, it is important to use a 10-weight oil in the fall and winter and a 30-weight oil in summer.

CHAIN TENSIONING

Even if your saw has been set up and serviced by a dealer, you will need to understand the very important factor of correct chain tension. Recognize first of all that all chains will stretch from day one throughout the entire life of the chain. You must be attentive to the tensioning of the chain at all times to prevent damage to the chain, bar and injury to yourself. When a chain is new, it should be snuggly fitted to the bar and just loose enough to be pulled along by hand (with the motor off!). Yet it should never be so loose that it sags along the bottom of the bar.

Tensioning of the chain is accomplished by first loosening the bar-locking nut or nuts half a turn to enable the bar to slide out as the tensioning screw is rotated. Next, rotate this tensioning screw, which is located on the front of the saw housing, in a clockwise manner. Once the chain is tensioned properly, lock down the bar nut or nuts securely to prevent loosening them while working.

A few words of caution here about chain tensioning. Chains must *never* be allowed to become too slack, for two reasons. First, a slack chain can come off the bar. If it does it can whip under the saw and against your hand or leg causing serious injury, as you can well imagine. Secondly, the part of the chain that will remain on the sprocket suddenly becomes stationary, but your sprocket might not stop turning for several seconds. In that time, it is entirely possible and very likely that the sprocket, continuing to turn, will chatter along the drive links of the chain severely damaging them. Sizable burrs will be caused along a section of the chain drive links and this will prevent them from sliding along smoothly inside the bar. The only repair for this is to replace that section of chain that is so damaged. This is a costly and unnecessary repair! It should not happen if close attention is always paid to the tensioning of the chain.

Another point to reemphasize is that new chains stretch immediately upon making the first cut with them. Be attentive to the slackness caused with new chains and always stop the saw to tension the chain whenever you notice slackness occurring. With new chains, this will have to be done after the first cut, after another four or five cuts and, perhaps, after the next dozen or so cuts. Attention to chain tensioning can save you a lot of grief as well as preventing injury to yourself or others.

Simple as the tensioning mechanisms are on all saws, it is surprising how many times owners are confused about them and how many times I have complaints from someone not being able to tension the chain correctly. It all stems from not understanding the mechanism. The chain tensioning mechanism is simply a pin located on the end of the tensioning screw that moves up as the screw is rotated.

The critical point is that this pin *must* be engaged in the hole provided for it in the guide bar. If it is, then as this pin moves up the screw it will pull the bar along and tension the chain. If it is not engaged the bar cannot be moved. So many times owners have not engaged the pin and have located the bar in such a way that when they lock the bar-holding nuts down firmly they force the pin into the housing of the saw, sometimes damaging the housing, and always bending the tensioning pin so that it either turns erratically or cannot be moved at all. Always be sure the tensioning pin is visible through the hole in the bar provided for it, *before* securing the bar nuts (Fig. 3-1).

The bar guide plates are another factor to be cautious of when setting up your saw. Most all guide bars will have an oiling hole drilled completely through the bar. It is through this hole that the

Fig. 3-1. When assembling the bar and chain, always be certain that the tensioning pin is clearly engaged in the bar hole provided for it before continuing to assemble the outside bar plate and the sprocket or clutch cover. If it is not properly engaged, the tensioning screw will be damaged when tightening down the clutch cover nuts.

oil flows from the saw oiler into the bar groove to lubricate the chain and the bar.

Two bar plates are provided with almost all saws: one fits to the inside of the bar and one fits to the outside. The inside bar plate has a slot in it to allow the oil to find its way into the guide bar oiling hole. The outside bar plate is solid and prevents the oil from escaping down the outside of the bar. In effect, it blocks the oil hole on the outside of the bar forcing the oil to be retained in the bar groove (Fig. 3-2).

If you are convinced that you have the bar plates on properly and the bar mounted so that the tensioning pin shows through the tensioning hole, you are now ready to put your chain on the saw. A chain saw cutting chain is a very complex and involved cutting tool. It is what has made the chain saw industry practical and effective. It is made up of a series of alternating left-hand and right-hand cutters, ground to a keen edge, held together by tie straps, and driven through a series of what are called drive links.

A chain will cut only in one direction. However, it is entirely possible for the uninformed to string the chain around the bar backward so that it will not cut. Without getting into an involved discussion of how to determine that your chain is on properly, let me describe it simply.

46

On all drive links of all chains there is a number. This is a model or type number that lets a dealer know the pitch, gauge, and size of the chain. It is sufficient to say that your chain will be on properly if these numbers on the drive links are showing to the outside of the saw. If the numbers are on the inside, or to the housing side of the saw, your chain is on backward and will not cut. Further, it will be damaged as the sprocket drives the chain from the wrong side of the drive links (Fig. 3-3).

Being sure that you have the chain on properly, string it over the drive sprocket and over the bar. Let it hang loosely and be sure that the tensioning pin is engaged in the bar. Put on the outside bar plate, then the bar or sprocket cover and bring the bar nuts up finger tight.

Tension your chain so that there is no slack at the bottom of the bar, yet never so tight that the chain cannot be rotated easily by hand. This is the ultimate test because in so doing you will get a clear indication of how much effort will be required by the motor to turn the chain. If it is too tight, the motor will labor. and all parts, including bar, chain, sprocket, clutch, and motor, will wear excessively to rotate the chain.

Fig. 3-2. The inside bar plate must be positioned so that the oil slot is visable. If plates are reversed, no oil will be able to get to the bar. The result would be severe damage to bar and chain.

Fig. 3-3. Numbers on drive tangs of all chains must be showing to the outside as the chain is placed on the sprocket and around the bar. This will assure that chain is always traveling in the proper direction. If the chain is put on reversed, it will not cut. But more importantly, it can be severly damaged.

At this point, I am going to contradict what almost every manufacturer recommends as to how to correctly tension your chain. In almost every instance, manufacturers maintain that when tensioning the chain the tip of the bar should be held up. I differ! I prefer to see a "natural" tensioning of the chain. Let's go back to the point where you have strung the chain around the bar and sprocket, located your tensioning pin, put on the bar plate and sprocket cover, and have brought your bar retaining nut or nuts up finger tight.

Manufacturers will say to lift the bar tip at this point and tension the chain. I say leave the bar alone and begin tensioning the chain now. At a certain point in the tensioning, the tip of the bar will lift ever so slightly. This is just at the point where all the slack is gone from the bottom of the chain. This is the point where I contend the chain is properly tensioned.

My argument is that if you lift the bar and tension the chain, if for any reason the bar is later forced downward (by cutting with the top of the bar for example), the forcing of the bar downward tightens the chain too severely, causing laboring of the saw motor. My method is an in-between determination. It should not be too loose if the bar moves upward and not too tight if the bar is caused to move downward.

STARTING A SAW

Once you securely tighten the bar nut or nuts, you are now ready to start your saw. Move your switch to the "on" position, close your choke lever or move it to the choke position, lock your throttle on and prepare to pull the starter cord through. There are three methods of starting a chain saw. One is the *drop method* and another is the *ground method*. While the ground method is safer, the drop method is quicker and less tiring (Fig. 3-4).

In using the ground method, you place the saw on the ground, put your foot through the foot strap to the rear of the saw and pull the starter through quickly. In the drop method, you hold the saw handle with your left hand and pull the starter rope through with the right hand quickly as you drop the saw away from you with the left hand. The danger in the drop method is that the starter might grab and cause the saw to swing to the side, sometimes starting the motor at the same time. Obviously, if the chain should come in contact with your body it could cause serious injury. See Figs. 3-5 and 3-6.

I find the third method best for me. I find a large stump, log, or box approximately 18 inches high. I place the saw on this and hold the saw down securely with the left hand. I pull the starter through with my right hand in what for me is a very comfortable manner. There is no bending way to the ground and no risks of being injured by a twisting saw (Fig. 3-7).

Fig. 3-4. The "ground" method of starting a saw. While this is the safer and recommended method, notice that the operator is in a somewhat awkward position. Another criticism I have of this method is that, as you pull upward, it is all too easy to straighten the back. This tends to put too much strain on the starter rope which causes ropes and springs to fail, especially if the operator is tall.

Fig. 3-5.This is the start position of the "drop" method of starting. The saw is held firmly with your left hand while your right hand holds the cord with the pawls engaged on the starter.

Fig. 3-6. Utilizing the weight of the saw, the operator suddenly pushes the saw downward and away from him while practically holding the starter handle motionless. The weight of the saw does the work for him and it is less likely to cause a strain on the rope and spring. Because there is a danger of the starting action causing the saw to swing against the operator's leg, this method is NOT recommended for novices.

Fig. 3-7. The stump method of starting. Notice the comfortable position of the operator. The back is straight and the left arm holds the saw securely while allowing a firm pull with the right hand. The only concern is to apply enough weight through the left arm to hold the saw securely and prevent it from swinging out of control.

As soon as the saw motor starts, you must quickly throw the choke to the "off" position. If you fail to do this quickly enough the motor will die. For the next pull at this point, always leave the choke on the "off" or "running" position. Another pull or two should start the saw. Next, trip the trigger. The throttle lock will spring back to the idle position and the saw should idle smoothly.

Chapter 4
Using a Chain
Saw in a Woodlot

Now that you have your chain saw set up and serviced, it's on to the woodlot. But where do you start? How do you best drop trees? And more importantly, how is it done safely?

In this chapter, the chain saw is examined from the most practical viewpoint—its actual use in the woods. I am going to deal with the "do's" and "don'ts" of chain saw use. I'm going to explain chainsaw safety and methods of dropping trees and bucking up the wood. I will give you advice that will allow you to not only walk into the woods with a chain saw, but also walk out with it after you're through—instead of being carried out!

I would guess that at least half of the purchasers of chain saws have never used a saw before, know nothing about cutting down trees and know very little about safety precautions in general. Many other saw owners probably know very little more about properly using a chain saw and they will probably continue to operate in an unsafe way.

There are some hard and fast safety rules that you should follow when operating on a woodlot. The first and most important rule is *never work alone*! If you insist on working alone, you are not only risking injury, you are also inviting disaster! A simple injury can become very serious if you are unable to summon help. A critical situation can be compounded into a hopeless event if you are alone. There is just no way you should risk the dangers of being alone in the woods with a chain saw.

Another rule to always follow is *never work when tired*. During a two-week stretch at my shop, no less than four customers told me of injuries they or their friends had suffered. *In each case* they recognized that the injuries had occurred late in the day when they had become fatigued and were just trying to finish up one last cut.

When fatigue begins to set in, it is much better to stop and call it a day. At least take a break and don't start again until you are sure you are rested and capable of working alertly. It is most important to be alert to all the potential dangers around you at all times. As dangerous as chain saws are, a chain saw has never caused an injury. It is always the operator who causes the injury.

THE BASIC CUTS

Let's begin with the basic cuts used to take down a tree. You have your saw serviced and ready to go. How to start the saw is explained in the preceding chapter. Now is the time to learn how to operate it. First of all, the grips are most important. Your left hand should grasp the top handle so that your left thumb is under the handle bar, *not* over the top. This will assure that your hand will not slip off and come in contact with the chain. It also assures you that the saw will not slip out of your grasp in the event you stumble or experience a kickback.

Keep your left elbow straight and locked to some degree. Naturally, you can't work stiff-armed, but your elbow should be tight enough to withstand any movement of the saw without allowing the saw to be thrown back at you. The right hand grasps the throttle handle with a firm enough grip to control the saw. If you have purchased a quality saw that comes equipped with a safety throttle, you will be required to grasp the rear handle with your right hand in such a way that the safety throttle is depressed before you can activate the throttle trigger with your fingers. With the saw held in this manner, it is unlikely that the saw will be thrown out of control unless there is a very severe kickback (Fig. 4-1).

For starters, you should pick a tree no larger than 8 inches in diameter. Even a tree of this size packs considerable weight and should be tackled with caution. The first thing you must do is determine the direction in which you want the tree to fall. A great many points must be considered here and they will be true regardless of the size tree you are attempting to fell. All things being equal, you must examine the tree to determine:

■ Is it leaning in any one direction?
■ Is there any excessive weight to one side of the tree (large branches, crooked trunk, etc.)?

■ Is there any wind?

■ Is there a clearing available in which to fell the tree?

Assuming that the tree is standing vertically with no excessive weight to any one side, there is no wind blowing, and there is a clearing in which to drop the tree, begin by making your *wedge cut* on the side you want the tree to fall. This wedge cut is very important and must be made accurately. The cut *must* be in excess of 45 degrees.

The reason for this type cut is simple geometry. A wedge cut of less than 45 degrees will close up as the tree falls. This will cause the tree to split and present difficulty in bucking up. Besides that, if it does split upon falling it could be extremely dangerous because there is no way of knowing where a split tree will end up.

Start your wedge cut by making the bottom (horizontal) cut first. This way you can stop when you get one-third of the way through the trunk. If you make the top cut first, you will not have as complete an idea of when you are one-third of the way through. Try to make the two cuts so that they join up accurately and do not overlap.

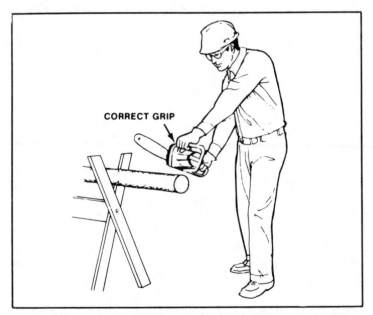

Fig. 4-1. The correct grip requires arm extension and stance for operating a chain saw. Notice that the operator is in balance, that his left arm is held straight and that his left thumb is well under the top handle of the saw (courtesy of Homelite, a Division of Textron).

As in all cases, a really sharp chain will be a great help here so that the cut does not angle off to a spot other than where you want it. Make your cuts at a point close to the roots of the tree and just above where the trunk begins to spread out to the root structure. It is always nice to cut trees as close to the ground as possible. But you can always come back to the stump and clean it up later. For now, and for the sake of safety, stay with the part of the trunk that is straight.

Having made the wedge cut, and having disloged the wedge, you are now ready to tackle the *felling cut*. This cut must be made on the opposite side of the tree approximately 1-inch above the juncture of the wedge cut. It should come through on a true horizontal plane.

As you start through with this cut, carefully watch the cut behind the saw blade. Notice with great care just when it opens up. You must also watch carefully the direction of your cut to be sure that you are cutting along the plane that will take you to the wedge cut at a point just 1-inch above the juncture.

Be prepared to stop cutting at just the moment the back cut starts to open up. This is an indication that the tree is tipping in the desired direction. The moment you see that cut start to open take the saw out of the cut, *shut it off*, and retreat along a predetermined path out of the way of the falling tree. If done properly and with care, the tree will start to tip slowly and gain momentum as it falls. See Fig. 4-2 for the sequence of wedge and felling cuts.

It is during the time that the tree starts to fall, and before it accelerates quickly, that you should make your retreat to safety. If you have done everything properly, the hinge that you leave will break off as the tree falls to the ground (Fig. 4-3).

A few words of caution must be given here. Although you must be prepared to stop the cut the moment you see the tree start to tip, you must be careful not be overly or hesitantly cautious. If you stop too soon, you might find that the tree does not go over. You will then need to reapproach the tree and carefully work away at the hinge until you cause the tree to continue on its way to the ground. This can be nerve-wracking and a little dangerous. It is better to make sure the tree is well on its way before you back off.

You *must* leave a hinge! If you cut completely through the hinge, the tree will do one of two things. It might settle right down on your saw blade and this will severely damage the saw or, what is more dangerous, it could spin off and fall someplace other than where you planned. This could be deadly!

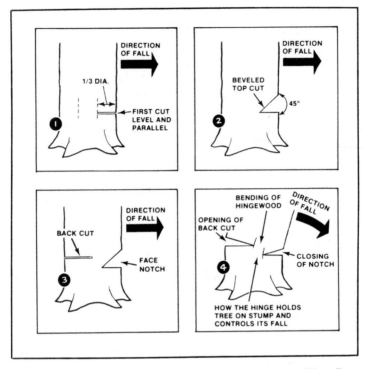

Fig. 4-2. The proper sequence of wedge and felling cuts (courtesy of Homelite, a Division of Textron).

The principles I have outlined for taking down an 8-inch diameter tree can be just as firmly stated for taking down trees with larger diameters. Regardless of the size of the tree, the basic guidelines will be the same. The larger the tree is the more careful you must be.

Another word of caution must be given here. When you look over a tree before you take it down, pay particular attention to any rot or decay around the point at which you are going to cut. Decay and rot might be an indication that the core of the tree is rotten and it might actually be hollow inside. Watch the chips when cutting such a tree. If you notice the color of the chips turning from white to dark red or dark brown as you start your back cut, you can assume there is some decay within the tree.

In cases like these, there is a risk that the rotten core of the tree will give way before you get to the holding hinge. The tree might break off in an unexpected direction before you are prepared to retreat from the stump. This kind of decay might be visible when you make your wedge cut. But because you should only go one-third of the way through the tree at that point, it might not show up. It would still be wise to examine your wedge cut for any indication of rot before you make your *back cut* or *felling cut*.

BUCKING AND LIMBING

If you have been successful in dropping the tree where you anticipated, you are now ready to limb it and buck it up into movable lengths. If the tree is a sugar maple or rock maple, for example, there will be a profusion of branches to be cut or cleared from the trunk. You must be prepared to take off the branches in such a way as not to bind the chain saw. You should analyze each cut before making it to determine if the branch will fall away from the cut.

Begin by taking off all the larger branches. Get them out of the way and clear the trunk to be left by itself. Start on top of the trunk so that in so doing you leave the trunk clear of these top branches (Fig. 4-4). It is during this part of cutting up a tree that most instances of kickback occur—and most injuries as well.

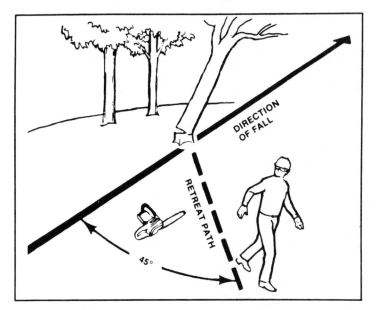

Fig. 4-3. The best path of retreat as tree starts to fall. Never retreat directly to the rear of the tree because it could get hung up in such a position that it will slide backward. Always have your path of retreat planned in advance and be sure to clear it of obstacles that could cause you to slip and fall.

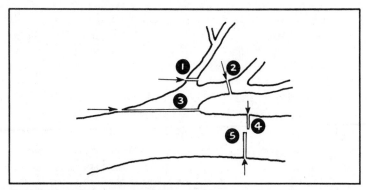

Fig. 4-4. A typical sequence of cuts in bucking up a tree. Notice that cuts 4 and 5 are to be made when a bind would be likely to occur if cut 4 were made all the way through from the top. Cutting in location of 5 from the underside (undercutting) will relieve the bind.

Kickback is a result of the tip of the bar coming in contact with a log or branch at just the point where the chain is moving in a downward direction. If it comes in contact with another log at this point, it will kick the saw bar upward and backward directly at the user. This kind of occurrence is responsible for the majority of chain saw related accidents. They are also the kind of accidents that are the most severe.

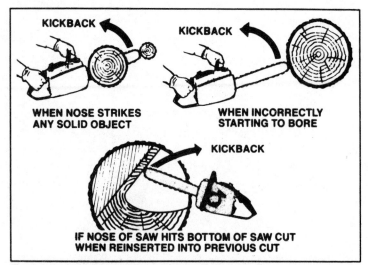

Fig. 4-5. Typical situation in which kickback will occur. The first example is the most frequent. The tip of the bar strikes an object beyond the log being cut. Attempting bore cuts as in the second example is inviting injury from kickback. The third example is often a real surprise and happens very unexpectedly.

The saw bar will react to kickback so very quickly that not even the seasoned professionals escape an injury. There are degrees of everything and kickback is no exception. I have experienced minor kickbacks where the bar was whipped up only a few inches or a foot or so. At other times, I am sure it could have been far more serious and could have come back at me striking my body, usually at the shoulder, arm or face. However, there are ways to avoid the dangers of kickback.

Kickback occurs when the tip of the bar comes in contact with a branch or other obstruction. The obvious precaution is to avoid such contact. *Never cut when another log or branch is on the far side of a log, positioned so the tip of the bar could come in contact with it.* This is the third rule for safety! See Fig. 4-5.

I will commend the manufacturers of Homelite for providing a safety tip for their saws. This safety tip is fitted over the bar in such a way that the tip of the bar cannot strike obstructions. The only fault I find with this attachment is that if you find you need to remove the safety tip to cut through a log with a diameter larger than the bar length, you will be tempted to do so for that cut.

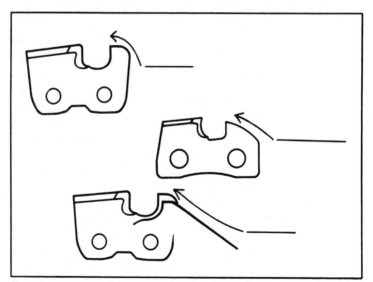

Fig. 4-6. A comparison of standard chain versus safety chains. The top example is a standard chain. As the raker enters the cut, the force of the entry is against the standard raker and results in a bumping action causing more frequent kickback. The second example is the low-profile, low-kick ramp depth gauge which minimizes kickback because entry into the wood is more gradual. Oregon's Guard Link chain (bottom) provides the smoothest entry and the least kickback (courtesy of Oregon Chain, a Division of Omark Industries).

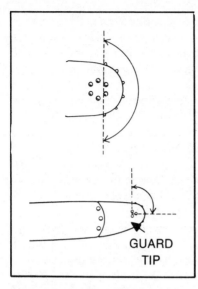

Fig. 4-7. These are standard bars (as opposed to safety-tip bars). The standard bar has a symmetrical nose configuration in which the entire periphery of the nose is subject to kick back because the chain is traveling downward throughout the travel around the nose. In Oregon's Guard-Tip bar, the downward travel of the chain is actually traveling back on the bottom of the bar and kickback is unlikely to occur at that point (courtesy of Oregon Chain, a Division, of Omark Industries).

GUARD
TIP

Human failings being what they are, you might also neglect to replace the tip right away. Who can say that a kickback might not occur at just the time you attempt to make "just one more cut" before replacing the tip.

I prefer to rely on safety chains and safety bars that are in operation at all times. Such safety chains are designed with built-in ramps on the rakers. These slide into the wood more gradually and

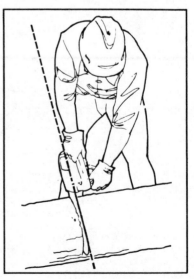

Fig. 4-8. When cutting, always stand to the side of the cut so that if an unexpected kickback occurs, the plane of the kickback will be off to the side with little likelihood of getting injured (courtesy of Homelite, a Division of Testron).

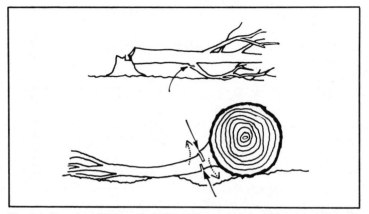

Fig. 4-9. Some typical examples of branches and logs under tension. You will have to recognize tension when it occurs and plan your cuts ahead so that you do not injure yourself or damage your equipment.

minimizing about 40 percent of the potential for kickback. When safety chains are utilized in conjunction with safety bars (banana nose or nonsymmetrical bars), there is a further minimizing of the kickback potential by another 40 percent or a total of 80 percent elimination of kickback potential (Figs. 4-6 and 4-7).

Most chain manufacturers produce and market safety chains. The Oregon division of Omark Industries produces safety bars to be used in concert with safety chains for optimum safety of operation. Athough in short supply at the present time, I suspect that in the future all saws will have to be fitted with these safer attachments.

Even if you try to follow the third safety rule about cutting, human failings must be taken into account. There are going to be times, try as we may, that someone will ignore, neglect, or overlook the potential danger of an obstruction to safe cutting. Under such circumstances, even the most careful cutter is likely to become injured. There is one more precaution we can all take to avoid injury from the possibility of a kickback and that is to *always stand to the side so the plane of a possible kickback will take the saw away from your body*. This is the fourth rule for safety! See Fig. 4-8.

Even when all possible precautions are taken, there is always the danger of something unforeseen happening. For this reason, rule one should be strictly observed—never work alone!

It should be easy to see that the most potential for kickback is in operations such as limbing the tree. Branches abound in every possible direction. All I can say is be sure to give careful assessment to *every* cut. Look behind every intended point of entry to be sure no obstruction is present that will cause a possible kickback. Cut to minimize binding of the blade and be most attentive to the danger of cutting when a branch or log is under tension.

Tension is another danger area of which to be particularly aware. While you are limbing, there are many times when at least some of the branches, and even the trunk itself, can be under stress or tension. Tension occurs when a branch is bent by the weight of the tree so that there is tremendous weight on it. It can be very near the point of splitting or bursting.

A saw cut at just the correct point will relieve the tension. A cut at the wrong point can result in the branch or tree whipping out of control, throwing the saw out of control, or causing the immense weight of the tree to come crashing down with very little warning. The possibility of injury to yourself or of damage to your saw is very great. Figure 4-9 is an example of branches or logs that are under tension. Also shown is the correct procedure to follow to relieve the tension.

Having removed the tree limbs, you are now to the point where you are going to start to buck the main log into movable lengths. There is a proper method to follow. I prefer to start at the top of the log by cutting off the sections so that the logs will fall to the ground without binding. *Always work to the uphill side of the tree* is safety rule five. Any pieces of the trunk that fall to the ground will roll away from you and not toward you!

In the event the entire log is lying flat on the ground, prohibiting you from cutting entirely through it, you might have to make cuts part way through the log. You will have to roll the log over to finish cutting it into useable lengths. There is also the possibility of a kickback when this is attempted.

As you cut partially through a large diameter log, the top of the cut might close on the top of the bar. This pinching action will bind on the chain at the top side of the bar and cause the saw to be pushed back at you. While not as severe a kickback as the tip striking an object, it can cause you to lose control of the saw. This danger is not to be minimized.

Another frequent cause of kickback occurs when the blade of the saw is reinserted into a cut previously made. This happens most often when you are taking down large trees or after you have disposed of the main tree trunk and have gone back to lower the stump. This type of kickback can be as severe as any other.

Perhaps the best means of minimizing potential injury is to be sure you have full control of the saw by properly stiff-arming with the left arm (Fig. 4-5).

UNDERCUTTING

Undercutting is the process of cutting to relieve the tension on a tree trunk or branch or of completing a felling operation when the tree gets hung up. Careful as we all try to be in assessing where a tree will fall, even the best of professionals will experience a hung tree from time to time. This can be one of the most dangerous woodlot operations. It demands extreme care, caution and skill.

There are correct measures to adopt when a tree gets hung up, but it is impossible to categorize each and every one of them because no two trees will act the same way in each situation. One of the most important considerations in dropping a hung tree is the angle at which the tree remains. If it is at an angle of 45 degrees, your procedure must be different from when the tree is hung up at either 30 degrees or 60 degrees from horizontal. However, the basic principles are the same. You must utilize undercutting.

One extreme caution must be exercised here. The tree you are felling will be hung up in another tree. Many novices will immediately decide that the easiest way to solve the problem is to remove the tree upon which the partially felled tree is hung. NO! This is the most dangerous approach imaginable!

There will be tremendous tension built up on that second tree. When you are employing the felling cut, it can be assumed that the pressure will cause the tree to snap wildly without warning at a point that cannot be predetermined.

It is far better to work the initial tree to the ground by utilizing undercutting or with the use of ropes, a winch or a peavy. Don't compound the issue by treating the result rather than the cause of the problem. Another very dangerous aspect of tackling the second tree is that you will be directly under the first tree when the second one goes and the results could be tragic.

Assuming the tree is hung up at 45 degrees, start by attempting to move the tree to the ground by using ropes or a peavy. Roll or pull the tree until it drops out of the obstructing tree. If you use a peavy, roll the tree away from you. If you use a rope, be certain you are far enough from the tree so that if it comes clear you will not be in the path of its descent.

If neither of these methods can clear the hang, then employ the undercut method. Holding the saw with a firm left arm, start your cut on the top of the tree at a point that is comfortable. This is called the *overcut*. Make your cut perpendicular with the tree trunk and *not* perpendicular with the ground. This overcut should extend about one-eighth of the way through the tree. Now come under the tree and with a firm left arm start your cut at a point that will meet the overcut, cutting with the top of the bar. The firm left arm is important here because the saw will want to push back at you as you cut. Pulling with an upward motion, make your cut until you are very near the overcut.

At this point you should slow down the cut and carefully watch the motion of the tree. It will break suddenly with the top portion dropping to the ground. if you want to be a little more cautious you can stop short with the undercut, remove the saw, and strike the trunk at the point of the overcut with a sledge or maul. This might break the trunk and let it drop to the ground.

This method is much preferred to the simple undercut method which can cause a trunk to split and sometimes bind the saw dangerously. Continue this over/undercutting until the tree has become disengaged from the obstructions holding it and drops to the ground. Then continue limbing and bucking as previously described.

In undercutting, overcutting, limbing or bucking, safety rule six is a must. *Never cut above waist height*. To do so makes the path of the bar so decreased as to make a kickback almost impossible to control. The most injurious kickbacks often occur when this important rule is overlooked. See Fig. 4-10.

SAFETY EQUIPMENT

Safety equipment should be used at all times. I would venture to say that less than 10 percent of the occasional users of chain saws own even the slightest piece of safety equipment. I'm referring to helmets, face masks, ear protectors, gloves, hard shoes, leg pads or pulp hooks.

There is no way of determining how many injuries could be avoided or minimized if all available safety equipment was used at all times. Safety equipment is extremely important and yet there is absolutely no emphasis placed on its use anywhere along the line—not by dealers who could recommend them; not by government agencies; and, most of all, not even by many professionals.

Recently I talked with a man in Connecticut who was a kickback victim struck in the face by the chain. He very nearly lost the sight of both eyes and was hospitalized for months. Even though he admitted that the use of a proper helmet and face mask would have greatly minimized his injuries, he was blaming the lack of a safety chain for his accident rather than the fact that he did not have and *still* does not use a helmet with a face mask.

Gloves, especially good gloves, can make an operation safer. Face masks prevent chips from causing momentary flinching and loss of saw control. Hard-toe shoes can be extremely important if a chain should accidently come in contact with a shoe. Leg pads made of many layers of tough fiberglass and nylon would minimize any number of leg injuries that often occur. There is no justification for not using safety equipment. I hope this book will cause the reader to be much more safety-minded.

Trees can react differently under varying conditions. Frozen trees, especially oaks, will have a tendency to split without warning. Any tree growing on a hillside or those leaning heavily to one side also present a danger of splitting while they are being cut. Be especially careful of these possibilities when cutting under such conditions.

Oaks are considered the most dangerous tree to cut simply because of their tendency to split. Professionals claim that oaks,

Fig. 4-10. Notice how the path of kickback is shortened when you are cutting above waist height (courtesy of Homelite, a Division of Textron).

more than any other tree in the woods, cause the majority of accidents in felling. Maples are more predictable because they do not split without warning as frequently. Pines also can be cut with a fair amount of predictability.

Oaks and maples that have a profusion of branches require more care when cutting because it is very difficult to judge just where they are going to fall. It is particularly difficult when you are standing among hundreds of trees—all tipping in various angles and with branches and limbs extending in all directions—to assess how straight one tree might or might not be. It is all relative and it is very easy to get confused and to incorrectly judge a tree's leanings.

In freezing weather, any tree can move quite differently than it would under warmer conditions. This is a very good reason for the casual cutter, who is supplementing his heating system, to get his cutting done in good weather. There really is no reason for you to be out in the woods during deep freezes. That's the time to be inside watching the Super Bowl!

Ash is another tree that will behave far differently when frozen and it should be handled with a great deal of care in the winter. When leaning, it can be a frightening experience to have one literally "explode" off the stump. Birches, on the other hand, will usually fall as predicted. However, the yellow birch has a large number of branches and presents the same problems as the oaks and maples.

There are some trees that are hollow in the center. They present a danger because they will fall without much control. Beeches and many soft "weed" trees, such as the larger poplars, will often be hollow and require very close attention when cutting. Apple trees are also notorious for this, but because they are not usually large they do not present as great a danger as the others mentioned.

SAFETY RULES

Here are the rules I have previously outlined in this chapter and a few more words of caution:

■ Never work alone in the woods.

■ Never work when tired.

■ Never cut when another log or branch is positioned on the far side of a log so that the tip of the bar can come in contact with it.

■ Always stand to the side of the saw so that the plane of a possible kickback will take the saw away from your body.

■ Always work to the uphill side of a tree when bucking.

■ Never cut above waist height.

■ Wear safety equipment such as helmets, glasses, gloves, hard-toed shoes, safety pads, etc.

■ Have at least two plastic wedges and an axe with you at all times.

■ Be attentive. Constantly think about and look for the trouble that might possibly occur.

■ Never cut on a windy day.

■ Be extra cautious when cutting frozen trees. Wait for better weather if possible.

■ Don't take chances!

Following all of these rules won't mean that you'll never be injured, but it will surely minimize the chances.

Chapter 5
Chain Saw Care
and Maintenance

In this chapter I will explain the care and maintenance of chain saws. Two facts need to be emphasized. First, a well-maintained chain saw is a safe saw. Second, any quality chain saw, properly maintained, can be a lifetime saw for the occasional user.

Let me state another truth from the viewpoint of a chain saw dealer. If owners of chain saws were capable of performing the *very simple* repairs that constantly surface, there would be very little need for chain saw repair facilities like the one I have run for the past 27 years. We just could not survive on the major repairs such as motor jobs, housing replacements and the like. I estimate that 75 percent of the repairs that allow me to make a comfortable living could be performed by any reasonably handy person if they have only the slightest bit of guidance. I hope to provide that guidance in this chapter.

I have adamantly maintained, and I tell every one of my customers the same thing, that if owners of chain saws would only learn to sharpen their chains properly—*and if they would do it?* I would be put out of business! I even take time to show them exactly how it can be done. I give them the opportunity to try it themselves. I recommend an easy-to-use sharpening kit. I correct their errors. And I try to emphasize how important maintenance is. Yet they still bring me saws that have had a lifetime of use put on them in just a few months because they insist on forcing dull chains.

The simple fact is that a sharp, well operating chain saw is designed to cut through a 12-inch log in 12 seconds. Use a dulled chain and that same saw will require 15 seconds, 30 seconds, and sometimes even a full minute to do the same job. A full minute would be five times what it should have taken! In one month, they have put five months' life on their saw and in a year they have put five years' life on their saw.

Is it any wonder that some users are constantly looking for saws with more power? They assume that power alone will enable them to cut through large logs. Any 2.7 hp or 3.0 hp saw will cut through any standing tree is it is operated properly with a sharp chain.

Another common problem I often see is overheated saws or saws with frozen motors. Just a cursory examination shows that the owner has used the saw excessively and has never bothered—or perhaps he was never shown how—to clean the packed and conjealed sawdust and mucky dirt from the cylinder fins. The saw will run hot simply because it cannot be cooled. I am paid a reasonable fee for repairing a malfunction that could have been avoided completely if the proper corrective measures had been explained to the saw owner.

I am going to try to put myself and other chain saw repair shops out of business by telling you just how you can get years more life out of your chain saw. All that is necessary is a minimum of effort, very little mechanical ability and no more specialized tools than you presently have on your cellar workbench or garage shelf. However, unless you intend to be more concerned or attentive than 75 percent of my customers over the years, you'll still be taking your saw to the repair shops around the country for the simple repairs you should be doing yourself.

STORING A SAW

For starters, I will assume that you have worked on your woodlot or at your woodpile for some period of time. You have cut down or bucked up 4 or 5 cords of wood. You are ready to put your saw away until spring or fall. What is the best way of storing the saw so that you will have a minimum of problems the next time you need to start it?

There are three possible alternatives for saw storage. One is to simply store it with the gas tank full or partially full. Another way is to empty the tank and run the saw dry. Neither choice is correct. The correct method is to empty the tank, run it dry and each month to 45 days put gas in the saw and run it for 5 to 10 minutes.

The first method will allow the diaphragms in the carburetor to become soggy and stretch. This will shorten the life and utility of the carburetor. It will also serve to clog the gas filter as the gas evaporates and this will leave a heavy oily sludge around it. The second method will allow the diaphragms to become dry and brittle, with the same shortening of life. The third alternative is very similar to a person jogging. It keeps the diaphragms in shape just like jogging keeps the human body in condition by working the blood vessels and the heart and lungs.

Another precaution recommended before storing the saw for a long period is to take off the removable parts and clean the motor. This involves removing the starter housing and the clutch cover. You will undoubtedly find the components, especially the cooling fins of the motor, with at least an accumulation of dirt on them. Take your saw to a gas station and use an air hose there to blow away all of this accumulated dirt so that the components are clean. At the same time, take off the air filter cover, remove the air filter and blow it clean (Fig. 5-1).

If there is any accumulated sawdust or dirt in and around the carburetor air box, blow that clean too—*only* after closing the choke shutter to assure that you don't blow the dirt into the carburetor air opening. At this time, also blow-clean the starter assembly so that your starter rotor will rewind freely. This is important because the air flow intake is located through the screen on the starter assembly.

Now you are prepared to store the saw for the summer or winter. Remember, don't use gasoline and oil that has been mixed for more than two months. And be sure to shake the gas can well because gas mix that has been standing for a long time will have separated. After the first fill, the mixture will be different than what a correct mix should be. Of course, the chain should be sharpened *before* storing so that if you need the saw for an emergency you will be able to go right to work. Don't wait until an ice storm has dropped a tree or branch across your driveway.

In many cases all of the above information might be exactly the way you have been caring for your saw in the past. However, I know some readers will find the information useful because each season I get dozens of saws that we must prime, start, and tune because they have been idle many months.

CHAIN SAW BASICS

As complicated and mysterious as a chain saw seems to be for many people, there really is very little that should cause confusion once you get familiar with it. Basically, a chain saw consists of a motor with a fuel system and an ignition system. The motor is basically a cylinder, crankcase, piston, connecting rod, and crankshaft. The fuel system consists of a gas tank, fuel filter, carburetor and the necessary fuel lines to transport gas to the motor. The ignition system is comprised of points, condenser, coil, flywheel, spark plug and the necessary wires to make the system function.

All of these systems operate to cause the motor to rotate and consequently spin the clutch and sprocket so that the chain is driven around the bar. A starter system begins the movement and the entire unit is covered by housings and handles so that it becomes operational.

Really, it is just that simple. If you don't let yourself become confused and frightened by what I've just said, you will be able to learn how to adequately repair your saw. Because I am going to stop short of getting into motor repairs (which must be considered major repairs) and housing breakage repairs (which are particular to each model saw), that makes it even more simple. That leaves only the ignition, the fuel system, the cutting attachments, and the starters. You see, it's getting easier all the time. Let's begin with the starter.

Fig. 5-1. Removal of motor housings will expose critical parts of a saw for periodic cleaning. It is important that all accumulated sawdust and dirt be blown or brushed away from motor cooling fins and electronic ignition parts.

THE STARTER

Although seemingly complicated, starters are really very basic. They are simply a housing into which a spring is coiled, which engages a rotor, around which the starter cord is wound (Fig. 5-2). The two areas of fear and confusion with starters are centered around:

■ Installing the spring into the housing and engaging it in the rotor.

■ Tensioning the cord so that it retracts after being pulled.

There is really nothing to it. After you've done it once or twice, you'll wonder why you ever paid someone else to do it.

The two most common causes of starter failures are:

■ Needing to pull the starter too many times because a saw doesn't start easily.

■ Pulling it too hard and thereby either breaking the cord or pulling it too far out and thereby staightening out either the terminal on the rotor or the anchor inside the housing.

Figure 5-2 shows a typical starter spring and the outside and inside terminals. In this first phase of starter repair, let's assume that you have broken a spring. The first step is to remove the starter assembly from the saw. Once you have this starter in hand, notice that the rotor will have a screw in the center of it. Remove the screw so that you can lift the rotor off the spring. Wiggle the rotor back and forth until you determine it has become disengaged from the center terminal of the spring. This will be obvious because as you attempt to lift the rotor out there will be a tension holding it back until it is disengaged. Once free of the spring, lay it on your bench.

If you have been successful at this, the spring will still be coiled inside the housing. Near the center of it, or near the outside end, you will notice a break if it is indeed broken. Use of a pair of duck-bill pliers is preferable at this point to lift the broken spring from the housing. Use care and grasp the spring securely to keep it from unwinding. If it does come loose and suddenly unwinds, you could be cut by it. Put it into a bag or barrel before allowing it to snap loose.

Almost all replacement springs will come wound to the correct size to insert into the housing. Replacing the spring is just a reverse operation of taking out the broken spring. Using the duck-bill pliers again, grasp the spring, as shown in Fig. 5-3, and insert it into the starter housing. Make sure the extreme outer terminal is engaged in the pin intended for it. All springs on *direct drive* chain saws are set into the housings in a clockwise direction (so you cannot make an error here). On *geared saws*, springs will be wound counterclockwise. Because only professionals use geared saws, I won't get into that area at all.

If you have been successful in placing the spring in the housing, you will notice the inside terminal has either a little hook

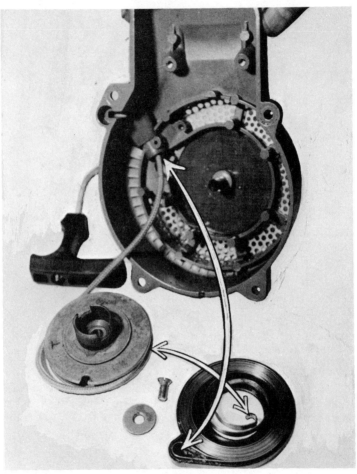

Fig. 5-2. A disassembled starter housing with a center post, spring, rotor, starter rope and handle. The outside terminal of the spring fits over the boss located just under the rope guide and is assembled so that it is wound in a clockwise direction. The rotor is placed over the spring so that a corresponding catch on its underside will engage the center terminal of the spring. While disassembled, the air screen on the housing should be cleaned of any accumulated dirt or sawdust. The spring should also be washed or blown clean.

Fig. 5-3. The proper procedure for installing a spring in the starter housing. Be sure the spring is wound in a clockwise direction. Holding it firmly with a pair of duck-bill pliers, locate the outer terminal securely over the corresponding housing boss before seating and releasing the spring inside the housing.

in it or a small round roll. In either case, it is this terminal that must be secured against the bottom of the rotor. Examine the rotor side to see just where you must place it to engage this terminal of the spring. Notice also that the rotor has an indentation on the outside edge. This notch is to be used in tensioning the spring so that the rope will rewind.

Before setting the rotor on the spring or into the housing, start the operation by winding the starter cord clockwise around the rotor until about 12 inches of the cord still hangs loose and is threaded through the starter housing with the starter handle outside the housing. Holding the rotor as shown in Fig. 5-4, place the rotor in the housing so that the terminal end of the spring is engaged in the hook provided on the underside of the rotor. As you place it down upon the spring, jiggle it around until it becomes engaged.

Try rotating it slightly in a clockwise direction when you think it is engaged. If it retracts when you release the rotor, you can be assured it is engaged. With the centering screw tightened on the rotor stem and a loop of the starter cord out toward you, use the rope to wind the rotor in a clockwise direction until you have made five rotations (Fig. 5-5). Holding the rotor at this point, use your left hand to pull the loop of starter cord out of the housing so that it runs straight into the rotor.

Slowly allow the tension of the rotor to take up the slack of the starter rope and, if you have put enough tension on the spring, it will rewind the cord entirely. If there is still some slack in the cord, pull up another loop to the inside of the housing and make one or more clockwise rotations. This creates more tension on the spring so that when you let the rope slide in it is entirely taken up by the spring tension.

The procedure is exactly the same for replacing broken starter cords. The only possible difference is the method of securing the end of the rope to the rotor. You will have to carefully notice how the rope had been previously secured and be sure to secure it exactly as it was. Replace the starter housing on the saw.

Fig. 5-4. Being sure the rope is extended out through the notch of the rotor, place the rotor over the center post of the housing so that the notches on the underside correspond to the inside terminal of the spring.

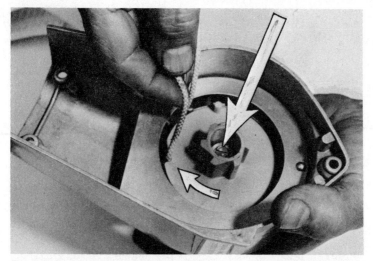

Fig. 5-5. Once the rotor is engaged on the spring, secure it in place with the screw and washer to the center post of the housing. To tension the spring, make five clockwise rotations. Use the rope to tension the spring as indicated.

Jiggle the rotor with the starter handle to be sure that it is engaged to the flywheel pawls. If the housings are flush, replace the holding screws and you're back in business. See Fig. 5-6. Now, that wasn't hard was it?

With very little exaggeration, starter repairs account for about 15 percent of my business. Common problems are pulled out ropes, broken springs, slipped springs, and broken ropes. What is really more important is that every one of these failures happens while the user is engaged in cutting with his saw. Naturally, he must stop cutting for the day, pack it all in, make a special effort to bring me the saw (or con his wife into bringing it down to me). In either case, it demands a drive of some distance, the inconvenience of delaying the job he started, and the harrassment of having to come back for the saw later.

None of this is necessary! With nothing more than a screw-driver or Allen wrench—and possibly a pair of pliers—every chain saw user should be able to rewind a starter or replace a broken cord. Of course, if the spring is broken you might need to buy a replacement. Broken springs are not prevalent; most times it is simply a slipped spring or a broken cord.

Don't be afraid to try to repair your starter. Just remember to do exactly as I have said. And if you fail, bringing it to your repair shop won't, or shouldn't, cost you any more than it would have in

Fig. 5-6. Once the spring is tensioned properly, replace the housing on the saw, jiggling the rope as shown to engage the starter pawls. When the pawls are engaged, you can secure the starter in place.

the first place. Tell the shop owner that you tried to save yourself some time and even go so far as to ask him to show you how to do the job properly. If you use a little psychology on him you might be able to flatter him into giving you a real lesson in rewinding the starter. If he refuses, you can always go to another repair shop next time or refer to this book.

Chapter 6
Troubleshooting
Your Chain Saw

Thomas Edison once defined genius as 5 percent inspiration and 95 percent perspiration. In the same vein, I have concluded that the troubleshooting of a chain saw is about 5 percent competence and 95 percent observation.

I can recall many times in my earlier years in the chain saw repair business that I labored long and hard over a repair that should have been accomplished in a fraction of the time. So many times the solution was right in front of me and I didn't see it. Many other times I just failed to look for the simple solution. Refusing to believe a malfunction could be very simple, I went all the way into a major repair only to find that the cause of the failure was very obvious if only I had looked closely.

I have learned through experience. Although I still make a few stupid mistakes, they don't occur nearly as often. After all, you've got to learn something just being around as long as I have. Observe! Look! Think about what you're doing before you take off the first screw, while you're taking it off, and after you've taken it off.

In this chapter, I'm going to make you an observer of your chain saw. I'm also going to guide you in a course of action that will make you start at the beginning of a repair and let you follow along, one step at a time, until you have found and corrected a malfunction. Then you will know to stop there and not continue until you have your saw taken down to a basket case. This course of action is not new. It's the way accomplished people work whether they're repairing chain saws or boilers. It's called "the process of elimination," "basic fundamentals," "troubleshooting," or whatever.

A chain saw can be reduced to a very simple mechanism. It is a motor which is fueled through a fuel system. It has an ignition system to ignite the fuel. It is started in motion by use of a manual starter. And all of these components work together to spin a clutch and sprocket that drives a chain along a bar, which in turn does the final work of cutting wood.

HOW A CHAIN SAW WORKS

Once you spin the flywheel of a chain saw (through the action of the starter), the action continues uninterrupted as long as the fuel lasts and if all the components work together to keep it going. If one component fails, it affects all the others. For example, if the spark is intermittent or fails, the motor stops. If the fuel system does not provide the right amount of gas, the action stops, etc.

As the flywheel is spun, each and every time it makes a complete revolution it provides one charge of electricity to the spark plug. Because the flywheel is attached to the crankshaft, it causes the piston to make one stroke inside the cylinder at the same time. Each and every time the piston reaches the top of the stroke, the ignition delivers the charge of electricity to the spark plug. There is a spark at the precise moment the piston is at its uppermost point. Meanwhile, the fuel system, through the action of the carburetor, has delivered a quantity of explosive mixture of gasoline and air to the cylinder.

At the moment the piston has reached "top dead center," these gases have been compressed to about 120 pounds per square inch by the action of the piston inside the cylinder. With the resultant spark provided by the ignition and the subsequent explosion of the gases, the piston is driven downward. Because there is momentum, the piston causes the crankshaft to revolve and the momentum of the action drives the piston back up into the cylinder again. The action is repeated all over again, with another charge of gas, compression of the gasses and a spark to continue the process all over again.

As the action of the piston continues, the crankshaft rotates. Attached to the crankshaft is the clutch. The clutch expands against spring tension—enlarging the faster it spins. As it enlarges, it contacts the clutch drum which is attached to a sprocket. The sprocket drives the chain around the bar and this results in the visible action we observe as a chain saw is used.

This is a very simple explanation of the workings of the 2-cycle motor that is in your chain saw. Now all you have to do is get this firmly in your mind and visualize what is going on within the saw. If you can do that, you will be able to understand my method of troubleshooting your saw.

Everything comes in degrees and this is perhaps most obvious when dealing with chain saws. If I could say to you that when ignitions or fuel systems fail, they fail—period, then my task would be simple. With chain saws, there certainly are times when components fail completely—when things are either black or white. However, there are many gray areas in chain saw malfunctions. Components don't always fail completely. Such malfunctions are most difficult to diagnose and correct.

When a chain saw is operating properly, it should start with no more than six or seven pulls. It should accelerate smoothly to high rpm's, come down to idle speed within two or three seconds, idle without quitting, accelerate smoothly again, stop when the switch is turned off, and start again on the first pull even when hot. When it fails to work this way, it simply is not operating properly.

I contend that every brand or model of chain saw built today is capable of performing as I have just described. I also contend that unless a saw is a total wreck, it is possible to repair any saw to perform properly. It is just a matter of diagnosing the problem, getting to the problem area quickly, and correcting it.

If the saw is malfunctioning where do you start? Many saws are brought to me by customers who are vague in their assessment of what is wrong. Many more are brought in with instructions to "fix it" or "it's just not running right."

When I do not have a specific complaint to go on, such as a non-oiling saw or one that does not start, etc., the first thing I do is to test the saw to see if there is anything obviously wrong. This means starting it with six or seven pulls, noticing the acceleration, idling, observing the oiling, looking for chattering of the clutch, inspecting the chain and bar condition, and generally making a very detailed observation of the entire saw. Somewhere along the line I will most likely notice a malfunction of some kind and then I can begin to correct what I find.

There are only three components that are basic to proper chain saw performance. They are *ignition, carburetion*, and *compression*. All three are essential. Without any one of them performing at 100 percent, there is bound to be some lessening of the efficiency of the chain saw operation. With this in mind, you want to start by first eliminating the possibility of a bad ignition.

My method of repairing saws, and it has worked very successfully for me, is to check for spark and ignition first—in all cases.

THE IGNITION

Ignitions come in three types: good, bad, and intermittent. A good ignition is one that fires properly with every stroke of the motor or with every revolution of the flywheel. A bad ignition won't fire at all. An intermittent ignition fires every now and then or becomes weak as it tries to perform. Come to think of it, it sounds like I'm describing myself here!

Testing an ignition is very simple. You can make a very positive visual test by simply removing the spark plug, reattaching the lead, grounding the plug to some part of the motor housing, and, with the switch in "on" position as you pull the starter through, you can see whether or not the plug is firing (Fig. 6-1).

A couple of words of caution here. Make sure you ground the plug well away from the spark plug hole so that any gas that might have accumulated inside the motor will not be ignited by the spark when testing. It is a good idea also not to ground the plug to the muffler for the same reason. With some saws, the only housings you will be able to reach will have been painted. You must be sure to ground to an unpainted surface because sometimes a painted surface will act as an insulator and not allow a spark or it will allow a weak spark. In such cases, it is conceivable that you might assume that you don't have a spark and you would perform a major ignition repair only to find that the spark was there, but the insulation of the paint prevented you from noticing.

With the plug properly grounded, pull the saw through. Each pull should cause four or five revolutions of the motor and thereby four or five sparks to fire across the electrodes of the spark plug. The sparking must be regular and it must be of a brilliant blue color. Pull the motor through at least 10 times; observe the sparking each time. If the sparking is regular every time, continues to be blue in color, *and* is a wide spark about one-sixteenth inch wide, you can safely assume that your ignition is OK. Reinstall your spark plug and go on to the next step in the process of elimination.

Once you have determined that the spark is OK, the very next thing to check is the carburetion. This also is accomplished with a very simple test. The test here is to bypass the carburetor by priming the motor. A common squirt can is very useful here. Fill the can with gas—the same mixture you are using in your saw—and before you reinstall the spark plug, squirt a couple of

Fig. 6-1. Ground a spark plug against the metal housing and well away from the muffler or the spark plug hole. With the plug out, the saw will pull over easily and if there is ignition it will show as an arc across the electrodes of the plug.

shots of gas into the cylinder through the plug hole. Put the plug back, reattach the high tension wire and attempt to start the saw, *with the choke in running position*. If the saw starts after a few pulls and runs until the gas you have primed the motor with is burned off, you can safely assume your problem is with the carburetion and nothing else.

When you test for ignition and the spark is nonexistent, intermittent or weak, you can safely assume that the problem is with the ignition. If you have made these two tests, found the spark to be good and sufficient, bypassed the carburetor, and still cannot get the saw to run, you will have to assume there is some problem with compression—the motor end of the saw. Compression problems come in three types: bad (worn, broken, or scored motors), air leaks (bad, broken seals or gaskets), and carbon buildup in the muffler area or exhaust ports.

REPAIRING THE IGNITION

A faulty ignition will cause a chain saw to either not start, not run consistently or run until hot and then suddenly quit. How can you make a quick determination of the trouble and repair it effectively? Start by checking the spark. As with every other method of checking a saw, observation here will be of utmost importance. With the spark plug grounded and the switch in the "on" position, pull the starter through at least 10 times. If the ignition is faulty, you might notice no sparking at all. You might also notice a very thin yellow spark or you might start with a good wide blue spark which, after a few pulls, starts to be thin and yellow or it might stop entirely. The spark might also be intermittent.

The first and simplest thing to do is to try a new spark plug and make the test over again. If the sparking now functions properly, insert the plug and your problems might be corrected. Suppose that the poor ignition is still obvious with the new plug. What now?

Now is the time to be especially observant. Look at the switch first. Try to notice if it is loose. That could cause intermittent switching. Switches on most saws will be either a toggle type or a button style. In either case, there will be a lead from the switch to the coil of the ignition. You will have to remove the housings to get at this lead. When you have done that, disconnect the lead from either the coil or the switch. Some have a slip-on style of connector and others have a screw type that is easy to get at.

With the switch lead disconnected, repeat the plug test for spark. With the switch lead gone, the ignition will always be on. If testing for spark now corrects the problem, you can be reasonably sure that the problem might be in the switch or the lead. Observe if there is a lot of caked dirt around either terminal of the switch lead or around the switch itself. Dirt can cause intermittent sparking too. Or you might have to replace the switch.

Let's assume you still have a problem after going this far. It's now time to look at the high-tension wire itself. This is the heavy, black wire that comes from the coil and has a rubber terminal that fits over the end of the spark plug. Pull it gently at the coil end to see if it is loose. In many cases, the high-tension wire is glued into the coil. If this is so, there will be little chance of it being loose there. However, on some coils the high-tension wire threads into the coil and can become loose. If it comes out of the coil easily, clip off about one-half inch of the wire and rethread it into the coil. After finding such a fault, you should go back to step one and test for spark to see if what you have done has corrected the problem.

Assuming a problem still exists, look at the other end of the high-tension wire. Inside the spark plug boot there is a little spring terminal that fits snugly over the end of the spark plug. This spring terminal can become loose from the wire or it can be rusty or stretched. In any event, this spring must make good contact with the spark plug or it will prevent a good spark. With a little effort, the rubber boot can be pulled off the wire for inspection of the terminal. If you do this, be sure that you hold the wire firmly to prevent pulling it out at the coil end. Once you have inspected or replaced the terminal, you can easily slip the boot back over the terminal by oiling the end that goes over the terminal end wire (Fig. 6-2).

If you still have no spark, now is the time to check the high-tension wire itself. Wires sometimes pass between the cylinder and housings to get from the coil to the spark plug and through use they can become charred or cracked. When this happens they will "leak" the electrical charge to the housing and this causes faulty ignition. There is a very simple way to "observe" this. Take your saw into a dark room and with the switch "on," pull the starter through several times. Observe the wire at the point where it passes near any of the housings. A "leaking" wire will show up as a spark between the wire and the housing it is leaking to. If this is the case, it is better to replace the wire. If you are far from a source of parts, taping the leak will suffice until you can replace it.

If you have gone through all of the above steps and the problem still remains, it is now time to start what can be termed a major repair of the ignition. This means repair or replacement of the points, condenser and/or the coil. These are components of a "standard" ignition. I will get into electronic ignitions later, but the large majority of saws presently in use have standard ignitions. Let's take those on first.

Standard Ignitions

You will find that the points are secluded in a "point box" which is located under the flywheel. Many times the condensor will also be located in this box. Other times it will be found secured to some part of the saw housing nearby the point box. The coil will be found secured to some part of the saw housing just off the side of the flywheel. There will be wires connecting all three parts.

The first step is to observe the coil *air gap*. The coil is mounted just to the outside of the flywheel and separated from it by an air gap of .008 of an inch. Before you remove the flywheel, observe the edge of it and notice if it appears that the coil is rubbing against it. If the coil has loosened from its mounting screws, it would move toward the flywheel because there is a portion of the flywheel that has a magnet built into the outside edge of it. When the coil comes into contact with the flywheel it will short out the ignition and prevent any surge of electricity to the plug—hence no spark.

At this point, you should regap the coil anyway to be sure that it is correct. This can be accomplished quite simply by use of an ordinary business card. Determine which side of the flywheel the magnet is located in and move the wheel until the magnets are directly in front of the core of the coil. Now insert the business card around the periphery of the flywheel and loosen the screws that secure the coil. If the gap is very wide, over .008, the core and coil will move toward the magnets. On the other hand, if the gap is less than .008, you will need to back the coil off in order to slip the card between the two (Fig. 6-3).

Once you have done this, allow the core and coil to move toward the magnet. Now secure the coil screws again and you will have gapped the coil properly. As before, if you found the air gap to be incorrect, it is now time to go back and test for spark again. No spark? Well then, you've got to go all the way!

You must remove the flywheel to seek out the points and the condensor. All flywheels are held on by a nut that is a right-hand thread and which will come off in a counterclockwise direction. The

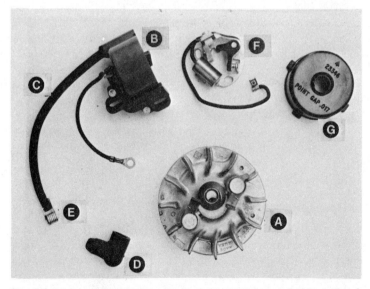

Fig. 6-2. The breakdown of typical ignition: A is the flywheel, B is the coil and lamination, C is the high tension wire, E is the spark plug terminal which is pinned through the high tension wire, D is the protective rubber boot which fits over the terminal and then over the spark plug, F is the points and condenser assembly and G is the point box cover.

Fig. 6-3. An example of the air gap between the coil and flywheel by using a business card when feeler gauges are not available. Place the card between the coil and the magnets of the flywheel. Allow the coil to be pulled to the magnet and then secure the coil in place.

problem of removing this nut is that as you turn it the flywheel and crankshaft also turn. You must be able to hold the flywheel securely as you turn the nut off. If you can hold the wheel with your hands, fine, but don't try crossing the cooling fins with a screwdriver. This is the best way I know of to break off the fins which are nothing more than cast aluminum in most cases. There is a much better and safer method called the clothesline method. Simply take a length of clothesline and insert it about 2 inches into the spark plug hole. Now turn the flywheel counterclockwise until the piston binds against the line. It will hold securely and safely now while you loosen and remove the flywheel nut.

Once you have removed the nut, you are ready to remove the flywheel. This can be the trickiest part of the whole ignition repair. Some flywheels are located to the interior of the saw housings in such a manner that they almost defy getting off. Others are somewhat external and are fairly easy to get at. Certainly the best method is to have a puller which is made for the saw and then these wheels can be pulled off with little effort and no damage. However, you are not likely to have a puller available. Flywheels can be "struck" off, however, if a great deal of care is used.

First locate the *boss* of the flywheel. This will be the heavy extrusion directly opposite the magnet of the flywheel. Laying the saw on the clutch side with the flywheel up, use a large screwdriver to pry the flywheel up as you strike the boss a good firm stroke with a heavy hammer. You can either pry slightly as you strike the boss, or, if you prefer, pull up with your hands while striking. I prefer to pull with my hands. If you do use a pry, don't pry excessively because pressure downward with the pry can sometimes damage housings (Fig. 6-4).

Don't be brutal in this performance, but you must also not be timid. For instance, using a small, lightweight hammer and striking the boss with many light taps will cause dents on the flywheel. The more strikes, the more chance of missing and hitting one of the cooling fins which can break off quite easily. It is much better to use a 16-ounce hammer and make one well-aimed stroke. You might need more strokes, but make sure that they are all firm, well-aimed hits.

If you cannot reach the boss with a hammer stroke, the other method is to strike the end of the crankshaft with a hammer. This method requires even more care. The first requirement here is that you rethread the flywheel nut back on the crankshaft until it is *absolutely* flush with the end of the shaft. Suspending the saw by one

Fig. 6-4. Striking the flywheel "boss" to loosen it. Use care to strike accurately and directly at the boss of the flywheel. Be especially careful not to strike the fins. They can be broken quite easily. Firm pressure upward with your other hand will pull the flywheel off as soon as the hammer blow loosens the wheel.

of its handles with your left hand (if you are right-handed), strike the end of the crankshaft with a good firm stroke just as before. In this method, it is much more important to make a firm and very well-aimed stroke. The hammer head must strike the end of the shaft absolutely flush! A series of taps will tend to damage the crankshaft threads more quickly. In any event, try to use a brass hammer for this as it will be less likely to damage the threads. Plastic or rubber hammers might do the job, but usually do not provide the shock necessary to loosen the flywheel (Fig. 6-5).

Removing the flywheel in this manner requires close attention to detail because it will not actually pop right off,—it will simply loosen. Many times it moves ever so slightly on the first strike. If you don't notice this slight movement, you might continue to strike the shaft unnecessarily after the job has been done.

Once the flywheel has been removed, the most important practice of observation comes into play. Without a doubt, you will find the point box packed with dirt and sawdust. Clean it! Learn to work as cleanly as possible all the time. If an air hose is available nearby, blow all the dirt away before proceeding. Before you do this, notice the key in the crankshaft that locates the flywheel on the shaft and be sure you don't blow that away when you are cleaning the point box area. Notice if the key is stripped at this point. Ignitions will fail if the key is gone or broken off. If you find this condition, you can be certain you've found the cause of the ignition failure. If the key is in place, remove it before using an air hose to blow the dirt away. Losing it could cause quite a delay in locating a replacement. See Fig. 6-6.

Once the point box is exposed and the area is clean, the first thing you must do is to take a quiet minute or two to study just what you are seeing. You will see wires coming from the coil and condensor to a terminal on the point box. You must remember just how these wires are located and secured. Draw a diagram if necessary so that you replace them just as they come off. Notice that the metal terminals of each of these wires are resting on a plastic piece on the point box so that no part of these terminals touch any metal. When replacing the terminals, it is of utmost importance that they not come in contact with any metal. Otherwise they will short to the housing and prevent ignition.

Also observe at this point if any of the wires are loose or cut. Either condition will prevent the ignition from functioning. After, and only after you have made all of these observations, are you ready to replace the points and condensor.

Locate and remove the snap, spring or screws that hold the point box cover in place and lift off the cover that will expose the points. Chances are that they will be dirty or covered with oil. In any event, obtain a new set of points and a condenser and replace them just the way you take them out. If you've gone this far, it is only false economy to try to clean or file the points.

Installing the points is not a really difficult job, but it does take a little guidance. Just like the coil, they must be gapped properly.

Fig. 6-5. The alternate method of removing a flywheel when the housing of a saw prevents obtaining a clear blow at the flywheel boss. The saw should be "hung" free with one hand while the hammer blow is directed very accurately at the crankshaft end. Notice that the crankshaft nut is perfectly flush with the shaft for this. This is recommended only in extreme cases where pullers are not available and a mechanic is capable of performing the job without damaging the crankshaft. If the flywheel is not dislodged with one or two good solid blows, refrain from continuing this method and seek the aid of a good repair shop.

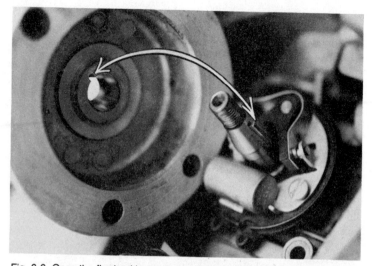

Fig. 6-6. Once the flywheel is removed, look closely to locate the key and the keyway. Notice that the keyway in the flywheel is designed to fit snugly over the key. Be sure that when you replace the flywheel it fits properly over the key.

You will notice that the plastic arm of the point set rides on the crankshaft. As the shaft is turned, this arm rides up upon a cam which is built into the shaft. This in turn opens the points. In operation, it is at this precise moment that the coil and condensor act in such a way as to cause a spark to jump across the points. The resultant charge is what fires the spark plug. The distance that the points open up is very critical and should be exactly .015 of an inch.

You will notice that one of the screws that secures the points in place does so through an elongated slot so that the points can be adjusted to the correct spacing. With that screw just slightly tensioned, rotate the crankshaft until the plastic rocker arm is located at its highest point on the crankshaft cam or where it opens the widest. The space between the two contact points *must* be .015. If you have a pair of feeler gauges, insert them between the points, close the adjustable point arm so that they are closed upon the feeler gauge, and secure the screw tightly. You will now have adjusted the points correctly (Figs. 6-7 and 6-8). Replace the condensor and make sure nothing is shorting out. The job should now be finished.

While I emphasize that the point setting is critical, and it is, most of you might not have a set of feeler gauges readily available. If this is the case, try to locate a heavier business card than you used in setting the coil air gap and use that in place of the feeler gauge. This will affect the timing of the saw, but it will be slight. In the event this is all that is available to you at the time, it will pass. It might not be perfect, but it should do the job.

If you have replaced all of the parts properly, you should now have spark. The only possible alternative remaining to be done if spark still escapes you is to replace the coil. You will have to obtain a replacement from your repair shop and install it (gapping it just as previously described).

Electronic Ignitions

Electronic ignitions resemble in shape almost what a coil looks like. They are mounted to the periphery of the flywheel just like the coil is. They serve the same function as do the points, condenser and coil of a standard ignition. Repairing electronic ignitions is a real snap. Usually all you need to do is obtain a replacement and put it on just as you might have replaced the coil. Gap it using the same technique, but gap it to .010 instead of .008.

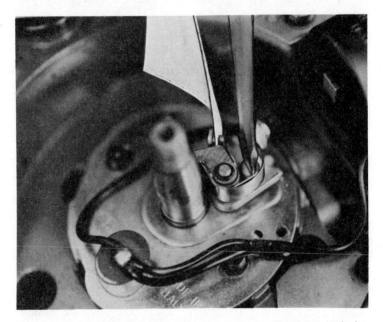

Fig. 6-7. Gapping the point setting using a business card in place of a feeler gauge. Because the gap setting here is just about double the thickness of the coil air gap, you will need to double the business card to obtain a setting of approximately .015. Use of a feeler gauge is preferable of course, but the card method will be satisfactory in the absence of gauges.

Fig. 6-8. This is what the gap of a point setting should look like after you have made the adjustment. Notice that the plastic rocker arm of the points is resting on the high point of the crankshaft cam. Once the crankshaft is rotated about a quarter turn, the cam action will allow the points to close while the condenser and coil act to store another charge of electricity throughout the next full rotation of the crankshaft.

You should make the primary tests of spark plug, wire, switch, etc., as I have previously explained. Replace the electronic ignition only after assuring yourself it is absolutely necessary. Electronic ignition modules cost in excess of $20 on many saws and they can be as expensive as $100 on professional saws. Don't jump to conclusions and go to that expense until you're absolutely certain it is necessary.

THE FUEL SUPPLY

Let's now assume that you have repaired any malfunction of the ignition and that it is operating properly. However, the saw still does not run properly. Perhaps you cannot start it or it takes many pulls to get it running. When it does start, it might race for a short period of time and then quit. Another symptom of fuel deficiency will be that when you depress the throttle, instead of taking off and accelerating smoothly to high speed, it either hesitates or actually quits. This latter symptom is perhaps the most common complaint due to bad carburetion and it is the easiest to diagnose and correct. All of the above symptoms of improperly operating chain saws are directly related to the fuel supply.

Before going any further, you should become familiar with the fuel system of a chain saw. By understanding what is involved, you can better make an accurate diagnosis of the problem and correct the malfunction. A chain saw fuel system consists of the following parts:

■ A gas tank.

■ A fuel pickup line that extends into the tank and takes the fuel to the carburetor.

■ A filter on the end of the fuel line, usually constructed of either felt or screen, to filter out dirt and debris.

■ The carburetor.

■ The gas cap, vented to prevent a vacuum buildup in the tank and/or a venting system to perform the same function (Fig. 6-9).

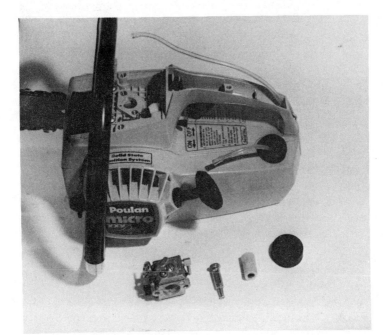

Fig. 6-9. Fuel system breakdown. Notice that the fuel line runs from the gas tank to the housing in which the carburetor is located. The other end of the fuel line rests within the gas tank and is referred to as the pickup line. The pickup with the felt fuel filter is located over the end of it. The carburetor and the fuel cap complete the fuel system.

Try to visualize just what happens. The gas tank is filled with gas. With each stroke of the piston within the cylinder, there is a compression buildup on the top side of the piston. When the piston is driven downward by the explosion caused by the igniting of the compressed gasses, it also accomplishes another function in the split second that it is being driven downward. In effect, it creates a vacuum on its way down which acts to pull the gas/air mixture from the carburetor into the cylinder so there will be another charge of explosive mixture in the cylinder ready for the next compression stroke of the motor. As the piston returns to the top of the cylinder, it compresses the gasses again, the spark plug fires again, and the whole cycle is repeated.

If the fuel system continues to supply the fuel required, the saw will continue to run. On the other hand, if there is a shortage of fuel, or if the mixture is wrong, the saw will not perform as it should.

Even though the carburetor looks quite complicated, don't let yourself become confused. In reality, a carburetor is nothing more than a block of metal with a series of orifices and passageways. Its only function is to take gas as supplied from the gas tank, mix it with the proper amount of air, and supply this mixture to the motor in the most volatile mixture possible.

We all know that gas will burn. Put a bucket of gas on the lawn and throw a lighted match into it and it will ignite with a "whoosh" and burn. Take the same bucket, empty the gas from it, throw a lighted match into it and you will get a faster and more explosive reaction. Why? Because you have leaned the mixture out. Instead of having 99 parts gas and one part air, you now have far more air and a lot less gas. If you were to take that same mixture and put it under pressure and throw a match into it, you would surely get an explosion. Don't try it!

This is the principle utilized in your carburetor. Through the series of orifices, passages, and primarily through the large passageway leading from the rear to the front of the carburetor (called the *venturi*), the carburetor takes raw gas from the gas tank, mixes it with the air being pulled through the venturi and provides it to the motor in a highly explosive mixture. The piston acts inside the cylinder to compress the gasses into a much more explosive mixture, about 120 pounds per square inch. When the spark ignites the mixture, there is the resultant explosion that drives the piston downward and provides the power needed to run the saw. It is easy to see how larger motors with more compression and larger carburetors create more horsepower and drive larger saws.

The principle, as just explained, should give you some idea of what is involved in tuning a carburetor. Two needles that protrude from the side of the carburetor regulate the air and gas mixture being sent into the motor. The needle to the housing side of the carburetor is always the low-speed control. The needle to the rear end of the carburetor is the high-speed control needle. Each of these needles controls the air/gas ratio needed to keep the saw operating smoothly at the function its name denotes. For example, when the saw is idling at low speed, the needle so designated must provide the proper mixture to allow the saw to idle. When the saw is revved up to high speed, the high-speed needle takes over and supplies the correct mixture to keep the motor running at high speed.

As with the bucket experiment on the lawn, if the mixture is too rich (too much gas and too little air), the speed of the explosions will be too slow and the saw will not come up to speed either on low speed or high speed. On the other hand, if the mixture in either needle is too lean (too little gas and too much air), the explosions will take place at so rapid a pace that the gas is burned off before more gas gets to the motor and the saw will stall at low or high speed.

Let's get back to the carburetor. All you need to know to properly tune a carburetor is that the low-speed needle controls the amount of gas being provided to the motor while the saw is idling. In addition, this needle provides enough gas to allow the *starting* of the motor to reach high rpm's. In other words, it provides a jet of gas mixture to the motor all the time. As the saw starts its climb to high rpm's, the low-speed needle must continue to supply gas in conjunction with the high-speed needle until the gas flow from the high-speed needle is supplying sufficient gas by itself to allow total high-speed operation without faltering, dying or flooding (Fig. 6-10).

When a saw hesitates upon rapid acceleration or dies, the fault can lie with the adjustment of this low-speed needle. The first thing to do is to open it a little and try the rapid acceleration again. When it is properly adjusted, it will continue to supply the proper amount of fuel for rapid acceleration and still allow the saw to idle.

On idle speed, the saw should idle at about 1000 to 2000 rpm's. As you lean out the low speed mixture while the saw is idling, the rpm's will increase. Enrich the mixture and the rpm's

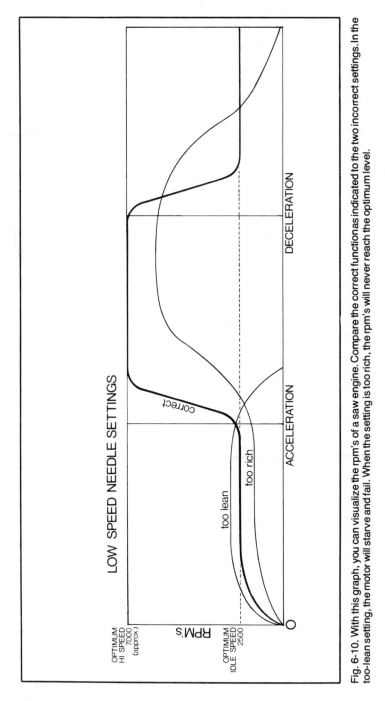

Fig. 6-10. With this graph, you can visualize the rpm's of a saw engine. Compare the correct function as indicated to the two incorrect settings. In the too-lean setting, the motor will starve and fail. When the setting is too rich, the rpm's will never reach the optimum level.

decrease. This is the bucket of gas on the lawn experiment all over again. Once you have the low-speed needle adjusted so that the saw will continue to idle properly at a speed just below where the chain begins to creep along the bar, you are now ready to take a crack at adjusting the high-speed needle.

The high-speed needle controls the gas mixture while the saw is racing along at high speed. Again, too rich a mixture and the saw will not reach the desired rpm's. Lean this needle out with the throttle fully depressed and the saw will race at a very high speed. But because it is being fed an insufficient supply of fuel, it will race and then die. Figure 6-11 shows what a high speed needle should do. It must keep the saw speeding along at its optimum speed without dying in the cut.

I recall one speed cutting contest we took part in a few years back. The previous year we had won three out of the first four places. This was primarily because we had sharpened our chains better than our competition. The following year we were determined to take all four first places. In preparation for the meet, we leaned our saw out until it was screaming several thousand rpm's higher than it was designed for. The saw was screaming along all right, until we put it into the wood—and it just died there! I felt pretty foolish as I walked away, but I've learned. I haven't entered a cutting contest since.

Other than a poor ignition, too lean a setting on the two needles is perhaps the most common cause of difficult starting. The correct starting point for both needles, if you have no idea of where the setting happens to be, is one turn open from closed on both needles. Close down the needles gently until they are closed all the way. Don't force them because you can damage the needles themselves or the needle seats. Then open them both one full turn. This general setting should allow you to at least start the saw. Then you will have to make the final tuning as described.

The idle speed setting is another setting that you must be familiar with. This is a very mechanical adjustment that simply opens the butterfly of the carburetor in idle speed. After you have the low-speed needle properly adjusted for good idle and quick acceleration, adjust the idle speed needle so that the chain just barely creeps along the bar. This is a very visual adjustment and it should cause you no real problem. Too high a setting here and the chain will continue to spin on idle. Too low a setting and the saw might stall on idle. All three settings must be made in concert with one another.

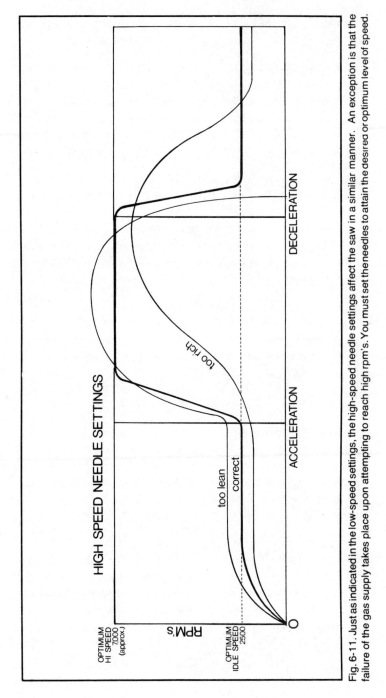

HIGH SPEED NEEDLE SETTINGS

OPTIMUM HI SPEED 7,000 (approx.)

RPM's

OPTIMUM IDLE SPEED 2500

too lean
correct

too rich

ACCELERATION

DECELERATION

Fig. 6-11. Just as indicated in the low-speed settings, the high-speed needle settings affect the saw in a similar manner. An exception is that the failure of the gas supply takes place upon attempting to reach high rpm's. You must set the needles to attain the desired or optimum level of speed.

First, set the low-speed needle so that the saw will not hesitate and will allow rapid acceleration. Then set the high-speed needle so that the saw continues to run at full throttle without dying in the cut, Finally, let the saw come down to idle and set the idle speed screw so that the chain is just below creeping on the bar. Always repeat the procedure, from low-speed to high-speed and then back to idle, to be sure you have the settings correct. If there is nothing else wrong with the fuel system, your saw should run properly (Fig. 6-12).

It would be too simple to say that setting only the carburetor will correct all fuel system problems. This is true even though they are easily responsible for a majority of the malfunctions. If setting the carburetor has not corrected the problem, and you still have less than maximum performance, you will have to look elsewhere.

Because fuel supply to the motor must be constant, it is easily recognizable that all components of the system must perform or there is going to be trouble. If you're thinking with me, you will immediately examine the fuel supply from the gas tank to the carburetor. This is the next place to look if setting the carburetor needles does not seem to correct a poorly running saw. With a wire hook or with your fingers, reach into the fuel tank and pull out the pickup line. It is a rubber hose about three-sixteenth of an inch in diameter (Fig. 6-13).

While you have the line out, follow the observation method I have advocated throughout this book. Look at the line to see if there are any cracks or splits on it. Put the line to your lips and blow back toward the carburetor to be sure that it is not leaking. It should hold air. If it does not, follow it along to the carburetor and determine where the leak is, correct it or replace the line.

Toward the end of the line you will see a filter that is made of felt or a fine screen. Take it off the line and try blowing a little air through it by putting the filter to your lips. It should "breathe" easily. If it does not, replace it or try cleaning it. Screen filters can be blown clean, but you will have to replace the felt type. Put it back on the line, drop it back into the tank, and see if this corrects a fuel starving problem.

When you are convinced that you have a solid fuel line and a clean gas filter, but still have a starving chain saw, the next place to look is into the carburetor itself. I will guide you in rebuilding the carburetor. This is a job quite frequently called for and it usually costs from $15 to $25 at most repair shops. More important is the fact that such jobs will require leaving the saw at the shop for a few

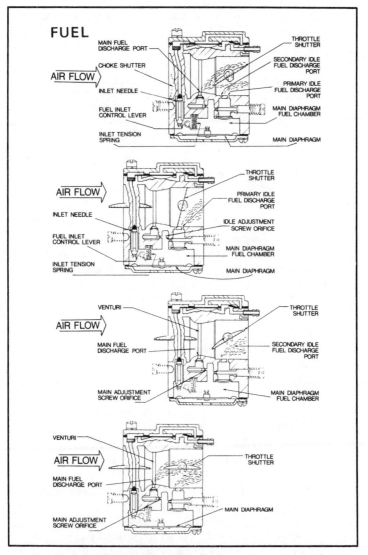

Fig. 6-12. In the top diagram, notice that when the choke shutter is closed for starting, both the primary and secondary discharge ports are providing gas to the motor through the venturi of the carburetor. In the second drawing, the choke shutter has been opened but the throttle shutter is not yet opened for acceleration. The saw is on idle. Notice that the gas is being provided through the primary discharge port only. The third diagram depicts the beginning of the acceleration process. The secondary primary discharge port begins to provide gas to a motor that is beginning its climb to high rpm's. In the bottom diagram, the saw is now running at top speed. All the ports are providing a maximum flow of gas to the venturi and thereby to the motor (courtesy of Walbro Carburetors).

100

days until workers can get to the job. There is really no need for this. You can do the job. See Fig. 6-14.

The carburetor, a little miracle of engineering, is the heart of any chain saw. You will have to take the carburetor out of the saw now. While you have it out, take a moment to look closely at it as you read this. It is a block of metal (aluminum) that is about 1½ inches square. It has a fuel inlet on the right uppermost side, two needles protruding from the lower left side and a large hole passing entirely through it from the rear to the front.

Inside the large passageway, called the *venturi*, you will notice two round metal discs. The rear disc is called the *choke butterfly* while the forward one is the throttle butterfly. Look inside the venturi closely. You will notice that there are three tiny holes to the front of the venturi at just the point where the front butterfly, or *throttle disc*, is. Somewhere back of these holes, on the bottom of the venturi, you will notice another larger hole, or round ball, protruding slightly into the venturi. Have you found them? Let me explain the function of these holes and the discs.

Fig. 6-13. The fuel filter can be fished out of the gas tank with a hook fashioned from a coat hanger. This will allow you to inspect the filter for fouling and, if need be, allow you to replace it. If you need to, you can remove the pickup assembly and test the fuel line for leaks by blowing toward the carburetor. If there is a leak, it will be immediately noticeable.

101

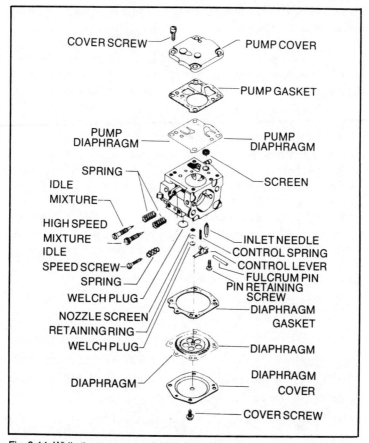

Fig. 6-14. While there are several different models of carburetors, this will serve to show you the parts of a typical one.

You will notice that as you pull back on the front accelerating butterfly lever, the butterfly swings from a closed (vertical) position to an open (horizontal) position. This simulates what happens when the motor is accelerated. The piston creates a vacuum in operation. You will notice, if you look closely, that this throttle butterfly is designed to close just between two of the small front holes. When it is closed, one hole is to the front of the butterfly and two holes are to the rear, or inside of the venturi. These holes are the low-speed jet outlets. Have you by any chance noticed that they are located directly above the low speed needle? You see, the needle controls the gas that is allowed to spew forth through these holes during idle speed and acceleration.

When this butterfly is open (or in horizontal position) all three holes are so positioned that they all provide a supply of gas into the venturi. As the action of the piston draws air into the motor, it must come through the venturi of the carburetor. The action that is created by this is very similar to forcing air over a straw with one end immersed in a glass of water. The passing of air over the straw pulls the water out of the glass and allows it to spray out with the flow of air.

The same thing happens within the venturi as air passes over these holes. It vacuums up the gas that is sitting just below these holes and carries it into the motor. As the accelerating butterfly opens wider, more air is caused to speed through the venturi. This causes gas to be picked up out of the rear two holes of this series and provides sufficient gas flow to allow rapid acceleration of our saw motor. Now the rear hole, the one that is back more in the venturi (the high speed jet), takes over. Notice that it is considerably larger in diameter. This is because it must supply a considerable amount of gas to keep the saw revving at high speed.

It only follows that any blockage of the fuel system could be located here within these holes. If after you have gone through the procedure I have outlined up to this point, and there has been no visible effect on the operation of a saw that has a fuel deficiency, cleaning these holes will be the next place to look. Use a fine wire for the job. The kind that comes attached to claim checks is ideal. Bend the end of one of these wires into a right angle with an end of about one-fourth of an inch. Sticking it into the venturi and down into each of these holes will clear any dirt that might be blocking them (Fig. 6-13).

Before you reinsert the carburetor and try it, you should replace the gaskets and diaphragms. You will notice there are two covers on the carburetor. One cover is on the top and one cover is on the bottom and they are held in place with four screws each. Carefully remove these screws and lift off each of the covers. Under the top cover, you will find a gasket and a rubber diaphragm. This is called the pump diaphragm. Under the bottom cover you will find another gasket and another diaphragm with a metal disc in the center of it. This is called the *main diaphragm* or *metering diaphragm*.

The metering diaphragm will sometimes have a little recessed ring around the pin that is located on the metal disc. This is designed so it will fit into the metering lever on the body of the carburetor. Turn the carburetor bottom side up and examine this

Fig. 6-15. Looking into the venturi of a carburetor from the motor end and immediately below the throttle butterfly, you will notice three small holes. These holes are the primary discharge vents and can be cleaned with a fine wire as pictured.

metering lever. It is like a little fork that fits over the recessed ring I just described. Notice that this metering lever is mounted on a pin that allows it to rock and that the other end of it controls a needle that is up under one end of the lever. Look straight up to the other side of the carburetor body and notice that there is a hole about one-fourth of an inch in diameter directly over this needle. It is through this hole that gas passes down by this metering needle.

The action of the metering diaphragm is such that as it fluctuates it will cause the metering lever to rock on the fulcrum arm. Each time it does so it allows a tiny amount of gas to pass through the metering needle. The gas is then passed up through the low and high-speed orifices and into the venturi. There it is mixed with the proper amount of air and drawn into the motor (Fig. 6-16).

The passage from the top of the carburetor block through the metering needle must be clear of any obstruction. Remove the metering needle lever and fulcrum and then the needle. Be sure that there is no obstruction in the passageway and especially at the point of the seat of the needle. Also inspect the screen that is seated at the top of the inlet to this passageway and be sure that it is not blocked with dirt or debris (Fig. 6-17).

Reinstall the needle, fulcrum pin and metering needle lever just the way you took them out. Make sure the lever can move freely on the fulcrum. Take extreme care that the forked end of the lever is absolutely flush with the body of the carburetor. If it is too high it will allow too much gas to pass through the needle and if it is recessed inside the body of the carburetor it will cause the saw to starve. It must be absolutely flush (Fig. 6-18).

Having obtained a diaphragm replacement kit from your repair shop, replace the diaphragms just as they came off. Be especially

Fig. 6-16. This shows how the metering diaphragm attaches to the forked part of the fulcrum arm. Whenever the fulcrum is forked, the diaphragm post must engage it. On some carburetors, the fulcrum arm is not forked. In such cases, the diaphragm simply rests against it during assembly.

Fig. 6-17. The inlet screen is located just inside the carburetor inlet fitting. Its purpose is to collect any dirt and debris that might find its way through the pickup filter. When a saw continues to starve for fuel, the inlet screen will be the most common area of blockage. It can be cleaned and replaced. When doing so, be sure the passageway below the screen and into where the metering needle seats is also free of dirt.

careful that the recess on the metering diaphragm is fitted properly into the fork of the metering lever. Replace the covers and you have completed a total rebuilding of your carburetor.

These two jobs, ignition and carburetion, cover the most common repairs generally done to chain saws. I would estimate that they comprise easily 75 percent of all repairs that come into my shop. But even rebuilding the carburetor can sometimes fail to correct a starving condition in chain saws. If you have rebuilt your carburetor and the saw still performs erratically, if it continues to act as though it is starving for gas, the only other place you have to look is for air leaks. A saw must be "tight." Air leaks can occur in several places and most of them are easily visible.

AIR LEAKS

The most common places for air leaks to occur are through the seals on the crankshaft. The seal most likely to be so affected will be the one behind the clutch. To get at this seal, it will be necessary to remove the sprocket cover of the saw and then the clutch and sprocket drum. All clutches come off in a clockwise direction. On some saws, you can remove the sprocket drum first and then the clutch. On others, you will need to remove the clutches first and then the sprocket and drum. Some clutches are held on by a left-hand nut. Some clutches thread onto the crankshaft and must

Fig. 6-18. The fulcrum arm must be absolutely flush with the body of the carburetor. If you need to adjust it either down or up, be certain that it activates the metering needle after making the adjustment. You might be able to freeze the needle in its passageway when attempting to bend the fulcrum arm.

Fig. 6-19. Using the clothesline method of freezing the piston inside the cylinder to allow removal of the clutch. This is the same method of freezing the piston so that you can remove the flywheel. The clutch will unthread in a clockwise direction. Not every saw will allow the piston to be frozen in this method, however but most will.

be driven off in a clockwise direction. Other clutches slide onto the shaft over a keyway, much like a flywheel. You might be able to remove them with a brass hammer in the same way a flywheel is removed.

Using a heavy hammer and a drift pin will remove the clutch. For clutches that thread off, use the clothesline method of securing the piston when doing this. Otherwise the clutch and shaft will spin. This will prevent you from being able to loosen the clutch (Fig. 6-19).

Once the clutch is removed, you will see the seal set around the shaft and into the housing. It will be obvious to you if it is leaking because there will be a residue of oil accumulated in the area most of the time. With a fine screwdriver, you will be able to pry out the seal. Replace it with a new seal and at least one of the possible leakage areas will have been corrected. (Figs. 6-20 and 6-21).

There is another seal located beneath or in the point box on the starter side of the crankshaft. If the seal on the clutch side has not corrected the air leakage, you will have to go to the other seal

Fig. 6-20. To remove an air seal at either end of the crankshaft, pry it off with a slim screwdriver.

and replace it in the same manner. To get to it, follow the same disassembly procedure as outlined in repairing and replacing the points.

If these two procedures still have not corrected an air leakage problem, there are only two other places to look. Your head gasket could be broken or the head bolts or nuts might be loose. By removing the necessary housing parts to enable you to expose your cylinder head, and with close examination, you will be able to

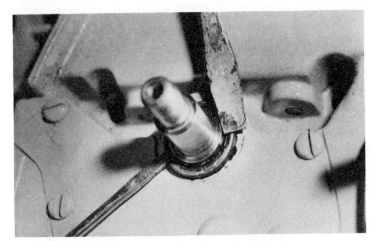

Fig. 6-21, Installing a new air seal. Be sure it slides into the crankcase housing squarely. Use any sort of tool that you feel comfortable with. Force it down until it seats into place. To make the job easier, coat the under and inner part of the seal with oil so that it slides over and down the crankshaft easily.

determine if your head is loose. If there is a large accumulation of oil around one side of the cylinder, you might be able to determine that the gasket is leaking in that location.

The only other place a saw will leak air is around the gaskets between the carburetor and the housings to which it is mounted. Close inspection and observation of any suspect areas will indicate if there is leakage. Look for loose screws, nuts, or broken gaskets. When you see a suspicious area, investigate it thoroughly. If your suspicions are valid, replace the gaskets.

I have purposely gone lightly on the areas involving air leaks because it is very seldom that you will find this malfunction. I know from experience that it will only happen about one in a thousand saws. More than likely, the other repairs I have discussed will enable you to keep your saw in the field operating effectively without ever getting into solving air leakage problems.

Leakage problems can be extremely varied from saw model to saw model. Ignition and carburetion problems are fairly standard in all saws. Almost every saw in existence will use the same Tillotson or Walbro carburetors. The only variations will be how they are hooked up to the throttle and choking linkages.

The same will be true in about 90 percent of the ignitions you will encounter. They will all be Wico or Phelon ignitions and there are some Bosch ignitions in some of the German saws. The variations will be with the shapes of the parts. Otherwise, the principles of repairing one ignition will apply to most of them.

The information I have passed on to you in this chapter will need to be assessed with some degree of discretion. Not all of the ignitions and carburetors will look exactly alike nor will they all resemble the illustrations I have presented. It will be up to you to use my information as a general guide and to adapt it to the saw you have. By doing this, you will help to decrease the business you've been giving your local repair shop.

OILING SYSTEMS

Oiling systems come in a variety of forms. These include automatic, automatic and manual, and manual only. All the manual systems are activated through the use of a plunger. However, there are a considerable variety of automatic systems.

There are piston plunger systems or systems that are activated by a gearing mechanism located on the crankshaft just under the clutch side seal. There are also geared systems that run off the action of the sprocket and other systems activated through pressure transmitted to the oil reservoir from the crankcase. This is the same pressure I have discussed that draws gas through the carburetor.

Because there are so many types of oiling systems, it would be impractical for me to try to direct you in repairing each kind. Let me try to generalize enough so you can at least make an attempt to observe the system you have. With keen observation, you should be able to reach some valid conclusions.

In manual systems, the areas to look for are the "O" rings on the stem of the plunger. Whenever you see an "O" ring that is stretched or broken, replacing it will improve the oil flow. The same will be true of saws that have both systems; look for the "O" rings first.

On the type of systems that utilize a gearing off the crankshaft, the same will be true. Try removing the oiling mechanism. You will notice most of them will have a series of "O" rings. Replace those that look bad. Move the parts by hand to be sure that they move freely. If possible, try to peer into the housing from which the oiler mechanism came from to see if the activating gear on the crankshaft is there or if it is broken. By pulling the starter through slowly, try to observe if it is moving. The gear on the crankshaft must turn in order to activate the oiler.

On saws like the McCulloch 300 series, the entire oiler is a plastic assembly that cannot be repaired in most instances. However, it only costs about $10 and the most practical recourse is to replace the entire oiler. On some Homelite saws, the oil tanks are pressurized. You will have to inspect to see that the check valves that allow a one-way flow of pressure from the crankcase are operating—and *only* in one way. This, by the way, is the only other area of investigation you can follow on many saws. There will be check valves located throughout the oiling lines.

Remove them and test to see if they perform in one way only. By exerting pressure with your lips to one end of the check valve, you will be able to blow through them, but you will not be able to suck through them. You must determine what direction the oil is flowing in and be sure the check valve is operating in that direction only. No check valve can allow air to pass in both directions. Simply replace any faulty check valves and the system has got to be improved.

On Poulan saws, the oil is forced through lines by a plunger that is activated with each stroke of the piston. These plungers are attached to a diaphragm much like the diaphragm in the metering end of your carburetor. Locate and remove the plunger and be sure that it can move freely in the hole. If the diaphragm is broken, simply replace it. Plunger housings will usually be found beneath the flywheels on all saws using this style of oiler.

Look into the oiler reservoir and fish out the pickup line much the same as the gas line in a gas tank. The oil line will also have a filter on it and you must make certain that it is clean and not blocked (just as you did with the gas filter). At this point, check to make sure that the oil lines are not loose, cracked or broken. If any of them are, you will have to replace them.

Without getting into a complicated discussion about each type of oiler, this is as much as I can furnish. I am convinced this information will be helpful if you will continue to be observant in each step along the way. Because oiling failure seldom occurs, I don't feel it would be practical to include a lot of technical detail. The most important general hints, I can pass on to you, in addition to what I have just said, is to work cleanly and to make sure that all your passageways to and from the oiler reservoir and the plunger and the pump are open and flowing. The use of probes and air pressure, plus the squirt can you used to prime the cylinder, will be helpful in clearing passageways. At least they will let you know when the passageways are blocked.

MUFFLER AND EXHAUST BLOCKAGE

Let me describe one more symptom of a malfunctioning chain saw that will sometimes escape the notice of many experienced repairmen. It is a muffler or exhaust blockage. The symptom of such exhaust port blockage is that the saw simply lacks power. You can rev the motor way up and it will not die like a starving saw. However, when you put it to the wood, the motor just seems to lack power. The rpm's come way down and the chain will stop simply because the revolutions of the motor are not sufficient to keep the clutch totally engaged. The first reaction of the user is that the motor must be totally burned out. That is just the way the saw acts.

Another telltale indication of such blockage, besides the reaction of the saw, is that the saw sounds like it is running under a blanket; it just sounds muffled. If you are always attentive to the "sound" of your saw, you might be able to pick up this failure quicker. Knowing what it sounds like when it is operating properly will help when it sounds differently and when the action of the saw is something less than optimum.

112

Whenever you suspect a burned out motor or a problem in that related area, the first place to look is inside the motor. The best way to look into the motor is to remove the muffler. Be observant! Look at the muffler to see if the baffles are clear or if the holes or screen of the baffle are blocked with carbon. Look beyond this point and into the motor. You will be looking into the exhaust ports of the cylinder. They should be totally clean of any carbon buildup and you should be able to see the metal periphery of the entire port holes. If the ports are blocked, what you will detect is a carbon buildup starting from the outside of the ports extending gradually into the port itself. The holes of the ports will sometimes have been diminished in size by more than half (Fig. 6-22).

When you detect this kind of buildup, you can correct and clean blocked ports simply by scraping away the carbon buildup. Be careful if you use a screwdriver because you can slip into the port holes and damage the piston. The use of a good hardwood stick like a popsicle stick is advisable. However, there are times when the carbon will be so hard that you can't dislodge it with a stick. At such times, you will have to use a screwdriver. Be careful not to damage the piston.

Be sure that the piston is totally blocking the ports when you scrape the carbon. This will assure that the carbon chips don't drop inside the cylinder head causing a binding of the piston. Whenever you clear the carbon in this manner, it is best to have an air hose available to blow the carbon away after you have dislodged it (Figs. 6-23 and 6-24).

CLUTCHES

A clutch is called a *centrifugal clutch* for a reason. It is just like a centrifuge. The faster it spins the more it enlarges within the clutch drum that houses it. Most clutches are made up of from two to six "shoes" mounted on a center (called a *spider*), which has a tension spring holding the shoes in a direction toward the center of the spider (Fig. 6-25).

The clutch is mounted directly to the crankshaft and spins in direct proportion to the rmp's of the motor. As the rpm's of the saw motor increases, these clutch shoes are then caused to fly to the outside against the springs that hold them in place. In so doing, they contact the clutch drum in such a way as to make a solid contact or "bind" within the clutch drum. The drum is part of the sprocket and so the chain is forced around the bar by the action of the sprocket.

Clutches don't slip! If used properly, a clutch will very seldom wear out. If a saw is always run at full throttle (and it should be), the clutch cannot slip in the cut. A clutch will only slip when the chain is so dull that no clutch can drive it through the wood. It slips then only because it is being asked to do a job that is impossible to do. A clutch can slip when the rpm's of the motor are insufficient to keep it totally depressed against the housing. This can be the result of running a saw at half throttle or when, because of a malfunction, the saw does not come up to speed.

Fig. 6-22. This is what a blocked exhaust port will look like. Notice the port orifices are almost totally blocked with a carbon buildup. Below the motor is a muffler screen from another saw that is also totally blocked with buildup. Either condition will cause back pressure in the motor and diminish the power drastically. On saws that use a muffler screen, the only practical repair is to replace it. In cases of blocked ports, the carbon can be scraped away.

Fig. 6-23. A slim screwdriver will allow you to scrape away the carbon buildup from the exhaust ports. Be careful not to mark the piston when you do this, but keep the piston in place as shown to prevent the carbon from being pushed into the cylinder. Use air or a washing means of flushing all the carbon chunks away from the ports.

Fig. 6-24. Exhaust ports after all carbon buildup has been chipped away and the ports have been flushed or blown clean.

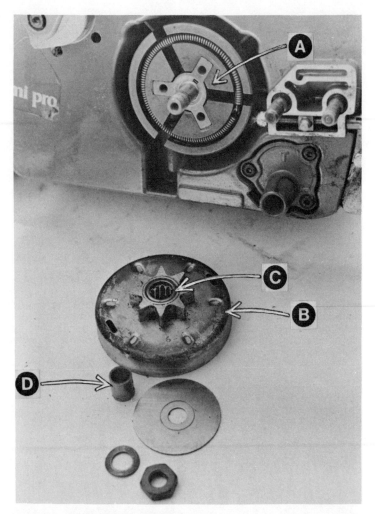

Fig. 6-25. A breakdown of the clutch and sprocket system. "A" shows a clutch assembly consisting of the "spider" in the center which is keyed to the crankshaft. Surrounding it are three shoes held in place by the clutch spring. "B" is the clutch drum and sprocket around which the chain is placed and which drives the chain. "C" is the sprocket bearing. This bearing should be maintained in a well greased condition. "D" is the race which slips onto the crankshaft first. It is followed by the drum and sprocket with a bearing. A large flat washer, a tension washer and a left-hand threaded nut complete the make-up of the clutching system.

I'll bet I see at least a customer a week who complains that his chain saw clutch is slipping. Customers often come in to buy a clutch from me to replace on their saw. In almost every instance I can trace their slipping clutch to a dull chain. Of course, nothing is failure proof and clutches are no exception. However, only about 1 percent of the suspected clutch failures are valid. Most of the time it is the result of the deficiencies I've just pointed out.

One way to prevent clutch failures is to *always* run your saw at full throttle. Doing this, and keeping your chain sharp, will eliminate most possibilities of so-called clutch failures.

When clutches do fail it will be the opposite of slippage. It will be a situation where the clutch is frozen in an expanded position. The symptom of this type of failure will be obvious when you try starting the saw. As the starter is pulled, the chain will travel around the bar in direct proportion to the revolutions of the motor being activated by the starter. Your saw will be very difficult to start and it will stall on idle. The reason for this is the clutch never "free-wheels." In other words, the motor is always driving the chain. This is true in the starting position as well as when it is brought back down to idle.

While this failure can be a frozen or broken clutch, it more often can be traced to a frozen sprocket bearing. If your sprocket drum is to the outside of the clutch, you can remove it and inspect the needle bearing in the center of the drum. It will be either very rusty or the needles will be frozen together. If you notice the needles are out of line, you can be sure this is the cause of the failure.

Many times these needle bearings are a separate cage of needles that can be replaced separately. Other times they will have

Fig. 6-26. Using a socket wrench of the exact size as the needle bearing, place it flush over the bearing in the sprocket. Locating the sprocket and socket accurately within the jaws of a vise, you will be able to press the bearing out of the sprocket.

Fig. 6-27. After removing a worn needle bearing cartridge, a new bearing can be installed using the same method. Hold the sprocket and bearing accurately and press from the flat side of the bearing. It is the flat side of the bearing that will have the model numbers stamped on it.

to be pressed out of the drum and another needle cartridge will have to be pressed in ágain. This is not an easy job if you do not have a press of some sort. But it is entirely possible to press the bearings in or out with a good bench vise. If you do attempt this job, always be sure to press on the side of the bearing that has numbers on it or the side of the cartridge that is flat. If you attempt to press on the rounded side of these needle bearings, you will damage the cylinder and freeze the needles. See Figs. 6-26 and 6-27.

If your clutch is to the outside of the drum, you will need to remove the clutch to get to the drum and the needles. Then replace the needles as described. Whenever replacing the needles or the entire drum, always grease the needles well before doing so. Many times you will have to replace the entire clutch drum when you find this kind of trouble. This should especially be done if you notice that the sprocket is excessively worn. This is a fairly easy repair to accomplish once you have obtained the proper sprocket drum.

Keep in mind that what I have set down here applies to any 5-cycle engine; lawnmower, outboard or brushcutter. Once you have become familiar with your chain saw, you should not have much trouble with any 2-cycle motor. Major repairs, such as motor jobs, have been purposely left out of this chapter simply because they only comprise about 1 percent or less of the repairs that bring chain saws to repair shops. It is the minor jobs that account for 99 percent of the down time with chain saws.

Chapter 7

Care of the Bar and Chain

The most important aspect of maintaining a chain saw is the bar and chain. About 75 percent of the repairs that come into my shop, or anyone's shop for that matter, are directly related to poor maintenance of the bar and chain. With no exaggeration, if my thousands of customers just practiced the principles I am going to set forth in this chapter, I would see my income drop to a quarter of what it now is and I'd have to lay off half my help! So if you are truly interested in keeping your saw working properly, read this chapter carefully and see for yourself how much money you can save and how much aggravation you can avoid.

There are dozens of manuals available on the subject of how to sharpen chains. Every chain package will usually include a sheet of instructions. Every owners' manual will have a section on chain sharpening. Every file holder and attachment will have some instructions on the subject. And yet they are either unclear, too involved, or in some way misleading because very few people are able to properly sharpen their chains.

Even after I sell customers a kit to sharpen their saws—whether it is a file for $1.50, a holder for $6.95, or a clamp-on device for $18.95, all with written instructions, and considering I will spend some 10 minutes explaining to them how to use the device—they still come back to me with dulled or improperly sharpened chains. Maybe I'm doing something wrong, but I don't think so.

The problem is that my instructions are either ignored, misunderstood, or not followed in the same way the instructions that come with all these devices and with every chain aren't followed. I am going to give it one more attempt here, and perhaps because you've paid good money for this book, you will keep it handy, refer to it from time to time, and comprehend what I'm going to say.

Look first at a chain and try to understand what it is and how it does its cutting. Figure 7-1 shows a section of chain as you would see it from the operator's position. The first thing you must notice is that it has cutters alternating left and right along the entire length of the bar. This is important because you must file the cutters from the correct side. Left-hand cutters are filed from the right side of the saw and right-hand cutters are filed from the left side.

SHARPENING THE CHAIN

Figure 7-2 shows a cutter by itself. The leading edge of the cutter is the part that does the cutting and it is the part that must be sharpened. Notice that there is a vertical plane to the cutter's outside edge and that this plane is just about 90 degrees from horizontal. *This* is the really important point to remember and this is where most people make an error in sharpening their chains.

It is very simple to maintain a 90-degree face. If you do so, you can be assured that the entire cutting edge will be properly sharpened. Notice that in Fig. 7-3, I have placed a file in the leading edge of the tooth. The file is positioned so that approximately four-fifths of the file is below the top plate of the tooth and one-fifth of the file is over the top plate of the tooth. This is very easily done if you use the proper size file and position it properly in the tooth.

Ask your saw shop for the proper size file for your particular chain if you are not sure what size to get. Table 7-1 shows the proper size file for each size chain. The real question here is, "Do you know what size your chain is?" That's why I suggest asking a good chain saw mechanic what size file you need. Then all you need do is keep buying the proper size after your's wears out. In Table 7-1, I've set down the correct file sizes for different pitch chains.

Aside from the positioning of the file in the tooth (which I call the *depth*), there is another important consideration and that is the *top plate bevel*. After you have placed the file in the tooth at the proper depth, you must angle the file at a bevel that will accommodate the existing top plate angle. But don't be so concerned with this top plate angle that you forget the important consideration—the depth of the file.

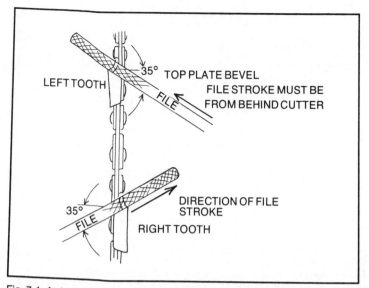

Fig. 7-1. A short section of chain looking from the top down. The teeth must be filed from behind and through the cutters.

I maintain that the top place bevel is certainly important to a smooth cut, but the *really* important concern is the *depth* of the file. You can be accurate in maintaining the bevel, but if the depth is off, the chain simply won't cut. On the other hand, I've seen many chains sharpened with the top plate bevels being way off. Yet, because the depth of the file was correct, the chains continued to cut.

Let me make one concession here to any criticism I will receive on this point. The manufacturers who build the chains have specific top plate bevels that they recommend. They will suggest that you hold your file at a 10-degree angle to accomplish a certain ᴏnfiguration of the cutter. They will insist on a 35-degree top plate ʳel, and so forth. All well and good! The occasional user reads all

ᵣ by itself. Notice that
ᵉ is just about 90
ᵉ critical angle to
ᵃ tooth.

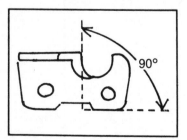

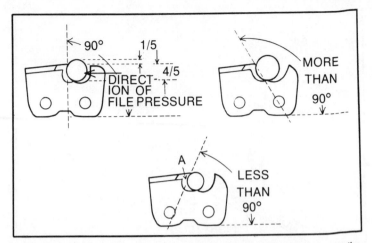

Fig. 7-3. The file should be placed in a tooth so that four-fifths of it is below the top plate of the tooth and one-fifth is above the tooth. This will assure a 90-degree face angle. Using too small a file or filing with the pressure downward instead of against the face of the tooth will produce a positive pitch to the tooth that will not stand up in the cut. Using too large a file, or holding it too high in the tooth, will cause a negative pitch to the tooth. The result will be an inefficient cutting tooth that does not bite into the wood.

of this, becomes confused, and forgets the very basic purpose of what to look for. Let's keep it very, very simple.

Forget holding your file at a 10-degree angle. Keep it perfectly horizontal. Forget to be overly concerned about the top plate bevel being exactly 35 degrees. Just concentrate on maintaining the proper depth—the four-fifths, one-fifth positioning of the file as I explained before. If you do this properly, all the rest of the sharpening falls into place.

Table 7-1. File Sizes For Chains.

Chain Pitch	File Size When Chain Is Full Size	File Size After Chain Is Half Worn
1/2″	1/4″	7/32″
0.404″	7/32″	7/32″
3/8″	7/32″	3/16″
0.325″	3/16″	3/16″
3/8″ extended or low-profile	5/32″	5/32″
1/4″	5/32″	⅛″

Begin by placing the file so that you are satisfied that you do have four-fifths of the file in the tooth and the file is on a horizontal plane. Now lean the file back to parallel the bevel of the tooth. This bevel may be 25, 30 or 35 degrees. The important thing to be aware of is that all the teeth have the *same* bevel. It is most important that the bevel of all the left-hand teeth be the same as the bevel you give the right-hand teeth. Being symmetrical is the key.

There is every reason to accept the manufacturers' recommendations about proper bevels. They provide a smooth cut and all the rest. Once you get really proficient at sharpening the chain my way, you can begin to get concerned about following the recommendations on the sheet that comes with your saw or chain. But learn the basics first. The most important basic is to be sure that the depth of your file is correct.

Now that you have been able to position your file properly, learn how to sharpen it. You must file through from behind the cutters, not into the cutters. The file must be *pushed through* the tooth in a very firm and deliberate manner. All of the effort *must* be on the front or leading edge of the tooth, with the pressure back toward the motor of the saw, *not* downwards! You must stroke the file with enough pressure to take metal off the tooth. This does not require a fast stroke. It requires a firm and deliberate motion the full length of the file. Never drag your file back against the tooth after pushing through. *Dragging the file will dull it immediately*. You should push and then lift the file out of the tooth for the next stroke, and push again.

Now you must consider what you hope to accomplish by filing the teeth. Some advice often offered suggests that you should count the number of strokes on each tooth and file all teeth with the same number of strokes. That would be fine if all the teeth were equally dulled or if you were capable of making each stroke identical. Neither case is possible.

You will notice, when filing, that it might be difficult to exert the exact same pressure on every stroke. There are many reasons for this. You are not experienced enough to do so and even the best of filers will find their file slipping on some teeth at some time. Most of all though, very seldom will all the teeth be equally dulled.

Ideally, and the manufacturers are correct here, you should choose the dullest tooth on the chain, sharpen it while counting the number of strokes it takes, and then stroke the identical number of times on each of the other teeth on the chain. If you want to do this, be my guest, but I prefer to sharpen each tooth so that it, by itself, is sharp, and then going on to the next one. After many sharpenings, you might end up with teeth that are much different in size. You must be prepared to use some discretion here.

If you notice the teeth becoming greatly different in size, you must attempt to file the larger ones to the size of the smaller ones. This is only common sense.

REMOVING DULLNESS

When manuals or manufacturers tell you to make the same number of strokes on each tooth, they are assuming ideal conditions and they are also assuming that you are experienced enough. It just never works out that way. What you must look for is to eliminate the dullness of every tooth. This takes some very extensive observation. You must look at each and every tooth closely and you must know what you are looking for. Very few people seem to be able to detect dullness.

You just wouldn't believe the number of people who bring chains to me complaining that there is something wrong with the quality or the hardness of their chain. They vehemently claim they are sharpening their chain every 15 minutes, but that it gets dull again after just a couple of cuts! The answer I must give them, is that the whole trouble is they have not been able to detect what dullness must be removed before their chain is sharp again. This is perhaps the most difficult to describe piece of advice in this entire book. In Fig. 7-4A, a chain tooth that is sharp is shown in contrast to one that is dulled (Fig. 7-4B). Dullness of a tooth can take several forms. You will have to look closely at chain saw teeth to determine where the dullness is.

Once you determine where and to what extent a tooth is dulled, the next step is to remove *all* of the dullness from each tooth. This may sound very elementary to a lot of readers, but it is just this inability to recognize dullness that causes the majority of saw owners to be unable to properly sharpen their chains. It is so simple yet so complex.

Consider a totally sharp tooth or chain to be 100 percent sharp. As the chain dulls, its efficiency is something less—say 50 percent. If in sharpening it you return it to anything less than 100 percent, the cutting efficiency will be directly proportional to that. If you get it back to 80 percent, then the cutting efficiency will begin at only 80 percent of its total capabilities.

What happens in actual practice is that when a chain that starts at 100 percent is dulled and returned to only 80 percent efficiency

Fig. 7-4A. The tooth on the left is sharp. Notice the keen edges to the top plate and especially the corner.

and then used again, it will dull more rapidly. The next time the efficiency might be down to 50 percent. If it is not returned to total sharpness, it will continue to dull even more rapidly. Soon the efficiency might be down to 5 percent or 10 percent and if the chain is sharpened poorly it will cut at that level.

The user thinks because a file has been run across the teeth a few times that the chain is sharp. Actually, cutting capacity might have only increased from 10 percent to 20 percent. No wonder the chain acts like it won't hold an edge. In reality, the chain has never had a chance because it was never brought back to 100 percent

Fig. 7-4B. The tooth has been dulled by hitting something abrasive. Notice the dulled leading edges; this is the portion that must be totally removed before the tooth can be considered sharpened.

sharpness. Each sharpening must return the chain to 100 percent sharpness to be an effective sharpening job. That is where all the trouble lies.

How do we determine when you have reached total sharpness? There are several things to look for. First, you must be capable of determining how dull a chain tooth is. This takes very close observation and a knowledge of what to look for. If you look closely under a good light, you will be able to actually see the dulled edges of the teeth. You must file across the teeth with enough firm strokes to eliminate every last trace of dullness. Don't stop until you have done so. Sometimes, depending on just how dull a chain is, this will demand as many as 20 strokes on each tooth.

A very realistic tip to pass on to you here is that you cannot expect even the best files to be capable of sharpening your chain more than six times before the file itself is too dulled to do the job. I recommend discarding a file after every six sharpenings. Using a sharp file makes the job that much easier.

Another recommendation is that after you have sharpened your chain about a dozen times yourself, take it back to your saw shop and let them put it on their machines to bring the cutters back to shape in the event you have been making any error in sharpening. Once back to the original shape, you are then ready to sharpen it another dozen times in the field.

THE FUNCTION OF THE RAKERS

Most chain saw users are unaware of the function of the *raker*. It's surprising how many times people refer to them as "cleaners." They think that the function of the raker is to clean chips from the cut. The actual purpose of the raker is to gauge the thickness of the chip that each cutter immediately following that raker will cut.

The raker must be kept .025 of an inch lower than the leading edge of the cutter. See Fig. 7-5. For comparison, .025 of an inch is just about the thickness of a match book cover. To make a chain cut properly, these rakers must be lowered to .025 of an inch below the cutter every two or three sharpenings. This is because the top plate of the cutter tapers backwards and, as you sharpen the cutters, you constantly decrease the difference of this thickness.

When the raker is something less than .025 of an inch below the cutter, you will notice that your saw is producing sawdust rather than chips. Not only does this make the saw overwork to produce the same results, but it is also just this kind of sawdust that will find its way throughout the saw to clog air filters, oiler orifices

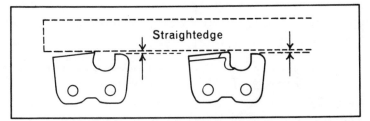

Fig. 7-5. Rakers must be maintained .025 of an inch lower than the leading edge of the cutter. A straightedge placed over two alternating teeth will show you what you are looking for.

and cooling fins. Keep a saw cutting chips and you will decrease your maintenance problems.

To lower the rakers you must use a flat file. File squarely across the raker top as shown in Fig. 7-6. Use a raker gauge if you have one. If not, use a straight edge as shown in Fig. 7-5. Determine with a feeler gauge or a matchbook cover just when your rakers are lowered uniformly throughout the chain.

It is superfluous to say that all rakers must be even on each side of the chain. If they are lower on one side, the chain will cut off to the side on which the rakers are lower. After two or three lowerings of the rakers, use the same flat file and round the leading corner of the raker so that it passes smoothly over the wood. Square rakers will cause a chain to chatter in the cut. See Fig. 7-7.

People constantly ask, "How long will a chain stay sharp?" This is like asking. "How far is up?" It all depends on the use you give the chain. In normal cutting, you can safely say, "A cord of wood per sharpening." Sure, you can do better, but there are many times when you will not be able to do as well. I've seen instances where a user has demolished a chain in minutes by cutting into an undetected stone, nail, bolt, or, what is worse, a block of dirt or sand in a tree.

You'd be surprised how many times this last incident happens. Where there is a yoke or crotch in a tree that has been catching dirt

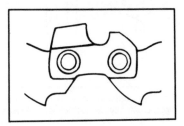

Fig. 7-6. The raker has been lowered by filing across the top of it.

Fig. 7-7. After lowering the raker, round the leading edge to insure a smooth entry into the cut.

for years. Just one cut into this kind of abrasive material is enough to seriously dull a chain. It is, in effect, a grinding wheel operation in reverse. Grinding wheels are made of abrasive materials, very similar to sand, with much sharper contours to the granules of the material. They are molded together to form a wheel and spun at about 6000 rpm's. When steel is put against it, it will grind away the material. A chain saw tooth is steel and turns at about 7000 rpm's. When it strikes a section of packed sand, the sand will wear away the sharp edges in moments.

This is especially true when you are cutting through a log on the ground. If you make the mistake of continuing past the log and into the dirt, you will dull your chain immediately. Most modern saws turn up at about 7000 rpm's. This means that some 500 teeth are passing any given point every second. That means your chain is making almost 90 revolutions every second. In one-ninetieth of a second you have given every tooth on your chain the opportunity to cut into dirt. It will take just one-ninetieth a second to dull your entire chain.

Even if you are an extremely careful cutter, you'd be surprised how many factors are working against you in the woods. Just for fun

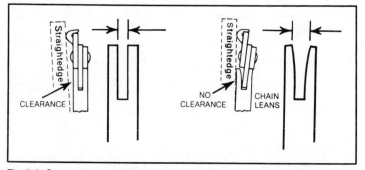

Fig. 7-8. Chains that are cutting true will abuse the bars. When the chain cuts off it will eventually cause the bar to be worn, as in the example to the right.

sometime, go out to your woodpile just at dusk and make a cut in a fresh log. You will be amazed at the sparks you will see coming from the cut. This is how chains become dull. It is impossible to say how long a chain will stay sharp. I sharpen my chain every hour when I'm cutting. That way the saw is never overworked. And because I'm basically lazy, I never overwork!

THE GUIDE BAR

Now, on to the guide bar. Care of the guide bar is almost as important as the chain. The only reason I say "almost" is because the guide bar is directly affected by the chain. Let me back up just a moment and say that while it is possible to sharpen a chain so that it is sharpened evenly, it is impossible to dull a chain evenly. One side or the other will be dulled more than the other. The direct result of this will be that the chain will want to cut in a curve. It will tend to "lean" to the sharp side.

When you attempt to cut through a 12-inch log, you will get into it about 2 or 3 inches and suddenly the saw will hang up. It just doesn't want to go any farther. Users will jockey the saw back and forth, up and down, and eventually force the saw through the cut. Their complaint takes the form of, "there is not enough set to the teeth," or that the chains are "not wide enough!" Neither is true or justified.

Chains are never "set," and it wouldn't matter how "wide" the cutters are. If they are dulled to one side and pulling to the other side, nothing short of accurate sharpening will correct it. The problem is that while the chain tries to cut a curve the bar will not

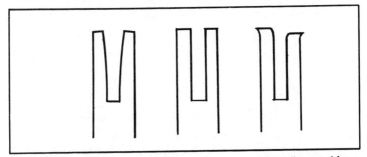

Fig. 7-9. Examples of damaged bars. The first has had the rail opened from cutting with a chain that leans to one side or the other. The middle example is one of a thinned rail caused by cutting with a dull chain. The third example is one that has had burrs produced from excessive heat caused when the chain leans one way or the other in the cut. The rails must be evened off by a bar shop or by filing (when practical). Simply removing the burrs will still leave uneven rails.

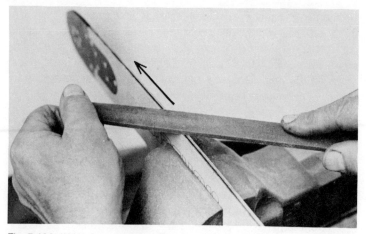

Fig. 7-10A. If you are a proficient filer, you can even your rails in this manner. Just remember to file along the bar, not across it.

follow! The result is that the guide bar takes the brunt of this abuse (Fig. 7-8).

If you continue to force saws through cuts in this manner, you will soon notice that one rail of the guide bar is discolored and burned. This "overheating" will cause the rail on that side to become soft and eventually roll a burr over on the side. Excessive abuse of this sort will also cause one rail to be worn thinner than the other rail. Now it becomes impossible to cut a straight line! Even sharpening your chain accurately will not correct it.

The only corrective measure to take is to have your bar squared up at your saw shop. If they have the proper equipment they can put your bar in quite good condition again at a cost far less than replacing the bar. Some saw manuals will recommend taking a flat file and filing off the burr to the side of the rails. This will do nothing to square up the rails. It simply gets rid of the burr. See Fig. 7-9.

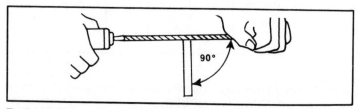

Fig. 7-10B. Try to even out any hollowed dips in the rail surfaces and to keep the file perfectly horizontal.

Fig. 7-11. Using the bar plates as a cleaner will allow you to keep the grooves of a bar clean. Be sure the oil hole is clear so that oil will pass into the grooves and lubricate the chain and the bar.

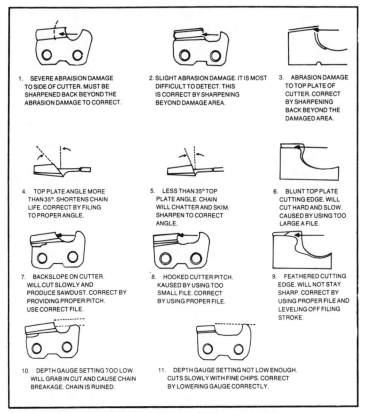

1. SEVERE ABRASION DAMAGE TO SIDE OF CUTTER. MUST BE SHARPENED BACK BEYOND THE ABRASION DAMAGE TO CORRECT.

2. SLIGHT ABRASION DAMAGE. IT IS MOST DIFFICULT TO DETECT. THIS IS CORRECT BY SHARPENING BEYOND DAMAGE AREA.

3. ABRASION DAMAGE TO TOP PLATE OF CUTTER. CORRECT BY SHARPENING BACK BEYOND THE DAMAGED AREA.

4. TOP PLATE ANGLE MORE THAN 35°. SHORTENS CHAIN LIFE. CORRECT BY FILING TO PROPER ANGLE.

5. LESS THAN 35° TOP PLATE ANGLE. CHAIN WILL CHATTER AND SKIM. SHARPEN TO CORRECT ANGLE.

6. BLUNT TOP PLATE CUTTING EDGE. WILL CUT HARD AND SLOW. CAUSED BY USING TOO LARGE A FILE.

7. BACKSLOPE ON CUTTER. WILL CUT SLOWLY AND PRODUCE SAWDUST. CORRECT BY PROVIDING PROPER PITCH. USE CORRECT FILE.

8. HOOKED CUTTER PITCH. KAUSED BY USING TOO SMALL FILE. CORRECT BY USING PROPER FILE.

9. FEATHERED CUTTING EDGE. WILL NOT STAY SHARP. CORRECT BY USING PROPER FILE AND LEVELING OFF FILING STROKE.

10. DEPTH GAUGE SETTING TOO LOW. WILL GRAB IN CUT AND CAUSE CHAIN BREAKAGE. CHAIN IS RUINED.

11. DEPTH GAUGE SETTING NOT LOW ENOUGH. CUTS SLOWLY WITH FINE CHIPS. CORRECT BY LOWERING GAUGE CORRECTLY.

Fig. 7-12. Troubleshooting chain and bar problems.

INCORRECTLY FILED CHAIN. CUTTERS ARE NOT EVENLY SHAPENED. CHAIN WILL CUT CURVES. CORRECT BY USING PROPER FILE SIZES AND FILING ALL CUTTERS SO THEY ARE EVEN AND SYMMETRICAL.

CHAIN HAS ABRASION WEAR ON ONE SIDE. THIS IS USUALLY FOUND ON THE RIGHT-HAND CUTTERS WHEN CUTTING CLOSE TO THE GROUND. WILL CAUSE THE CHAIN TO CUT CURVES TO THE OPPOSITE SIDE OF THE ABRASION DAMAGE. CORRECT BY ELIMINATING ALL THE ABRASION WEAR TO THE TEETH AND BY LOWERING THE RAKERS CORRESPONDINGLY TO PROVIDE CORRECT DEPTH GAUGE SETTING TO THOSE TEETH.

INCORRECT RAKER SETTINGS WILL CAUSE A CHAIN TO CUT RAGGED AND WILL LEAN TO THE SIDE WITH THE LOWEST RAKER SETTINGS. IF RAKERS ARE TOO LOW, THE CHAIN MIGHT BE BEYOND REPAIR.

Fig. 7-13. Troubleshooting chain problems.

If you do not have a quality saw shop to turn to, you can try to square the rails yourself. Put the bar in a vise and, using a large 10-inch bastard file, file along the rails as shown in Figs. 7-10A and 7-10B. Notice that the file is held at an angle to the rails and that the stroke is from end to end, not across the rails! This is called *draw filing* and it will result in ample stock being taken off both rails at the same time. If you are a proficient filer, you can do a fairly good job of squaring the rails in this fashion. This will only be effective if you catch the rails when you first notice a burr on one side. Badly worn rails cannot be corrected this way. They must be processed at a bar shop to be properly squared.

This is about as much as occasional users can do in correcting abused bars. If you are careful and attentive to the sharpening of the chain and if you will square the rails when they begin to become worn, you can save yourself a lot of aggravation and money. A chain in poorly conditioned bars will badly abuse the chain and this will result in necessary replacement of the bar and the chain. Both costly replacements can be avoided with a little care.

After each day's use, the bar should be removed and the groove should be cleaned of all accumulated dirt and debris. This can be accomplished by using one of the bar plates as a scraping tool (Fig. 7-11). Scrape all the dirt from inside the grooves. Take particular care to assure that the oiling holes are not packed with dirt. You should be able to look down into the groove of the bar and see no dirt at all. After clearing all the dirt, always reverse the bar so that you keep the wear on both edges even. It is the bottom of the bar that takes all the abuse of cutting. By periodically reversing

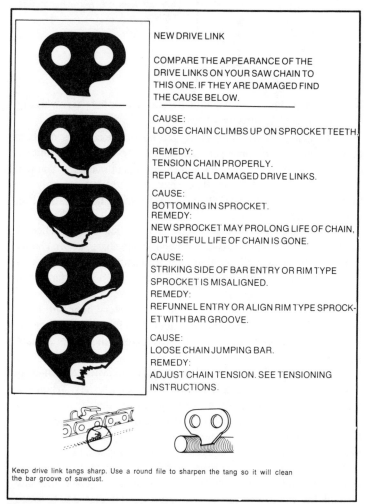

Fig. 7-14. Drive link problems.

133

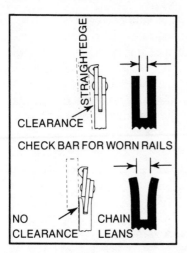

CLEARANCE

CHECK BAR FOR WORN RAILS

STRAIGHTEDGE

NO CLEARANCE

CHAIN LEANS

Fig. 7-15. Place a straightedge against side of bar and one cutter. If there is clearance between bar and straightedge, the bar rails are good. If chain leans and there is no clearance between bar and straightedge, the bar rails are worn. Bar needs replacement.

the bar, you will more than double the life of a bar before reworking or replacement will become necessary.

In Figs. 7-12 to 7-14, there are several examples of chain tooth dullness and bar wear. These are the standard examples found in most owners' manuals and chain and bar manuals. You will find them more useful now that I have pointed out not only the failing themselves, but also the reasons for these failings. See Fig. 7-15 and 7-16.

In concluding this chapter on bar and chain maintenance, I must reemphasize the need to keep your chain sharp. Sharp chains can make working with a chain saw a pleasurable and effortless event. Trying to cut with dulled chains is a wearying and aggravating experience. It is far better to sharpen your chains too often than too little. Sharpening your chain every hour will keep your saw out of the shop 10 times longer. It is the starting place for all maintenance work and it can greatly extend the life of a chain saw.

Many times I am asked, "How can I tell when my chain is dull?" I often reply by comparing this to carving a turkey. When you find you need to exert any extra effort to cut the meat, you can conclude that either the meat is very tough or that the knife is dull. It's usually the knife. It is the same with a chain saw. However, most of the trees you will be cutting for firewood will be hardwood trees that are pretty much the same as far as hardness if concerned. When you find that it requires extreme effort to force the saw through the wood, you can be absolutely certain that is is because the chain is dull.

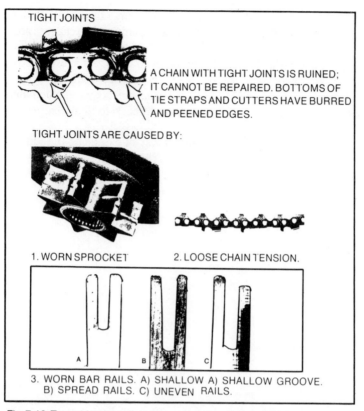

TIGHT JOINTS

A CHAIN WITH TIGHT JOINTS IS RUINED; IT CANNOT BE REPAIRED. BOTTOMS OF TIE STRAPS AND CUTTERS HAVE BURRED AND PEENED EDGES.

TIGHT JOINTS ARE CAUSED BY:

1. WORN SPROCKET   2. LOOSE CHAIN TENSION.

3. WORN BAR RAILS. A) SHALLOW A) SHALLOW GROOVE. B) SPREAD RAILS. C) UNEVEN RAILS.

Fig. 7-16. To avoid tight joints: 1. Always install a new sprocket with a new chain. 2. Keep the chain correctly tensioned and sharpened. 3. Take the bar to a qualified bar repair service for repair or replacement (courtesy of Oregon Chain, a Division of Omark Industries).

I never wait that long. I sharpen my chains so frequently that I never experience the need to force the saw through. And don't assume that sharpening the chain frequently will wear it out faster; the opposite is true. Sharpening a chain frequently will require no more than five or six strokes per tooth to get them all back to 100 percent efficiency. And if you do it frequently, you will discover that you will be keeping all the teeth pretty much the same size. Five or six strokes per tooth will mean that you are removing only about .0001 of an inch of stock from each tooth each time. Let the chain accumulate even the slightest amount of dullness and, if you continue to use it in a dulled condition, it dulls ever more rapidly.

Sharpening my chain every hour and removing .0001 thousandths of an inch of stock each time will result in the removal of

.0010 of stock in 10 sharpenings or in 10 hours of work. Work the same chain for 10 hours without ever sharpening it and chances are you will need to remove far more stock than .0010 of an inch. It will more likely be in the neighborhood of .0030. Continue the two chains side-by-side for another hour, and where I would then have removed a total of .0011, the dulled chain will require something like .0040 of stock removal to be brought back to total sharpness again.

It is easy to see that the surest way of extending the life of your chain and your saw is to sharpen the chain frequently. If you get nothing more from this book it will have been worth the price.

Chapter 8
Woodlot Management

In dealing with many chain saw buyers, I see a whole new generation of woodlot owners. Many purchasers of chain saws tell me that they have also purchased woodlots—either in the true form or in the form of a building lot. In many cases, they have purchased several acres and plan to clear some of it for a home site while retaining the remainder for a woodlot. Others have simply bought land for a wood supply and know very little about how to get the most out of it. As is the case with their chain saws, they are first time users of the woodlot. And, as with the saw, they really have very little knowledge of just where to start and how to go about it.

A good starting point for those who have just purchased some land is to seek out their county forester. Every county in the Northeast has a forester available to its residents. Many counties will also have an extension service available through state university systems and a county soil conservation district run in conjunction with the Soil Conservation Service.

Most counties will also have a county improvement agency and a regional planning agency listed in the major phone directories. A phone call to any of these agencies will be useful in easily locating your county forester. If none of these agencies are listed in your directory, the information operator can usually direct you to the right people.

Once you have reached your county forester, you will have to make an appointment to have your woodlot inspected. You will learn the best way to manage your lot by having the forester indicate which trees can be used for timber, which ones to cut for firewood, and which ones to save for wildlife purposes or future use. You will also receive advice on how to clean up and "sanitize" your stand to control insect infestation and weed growth.

If you have any valuable timber growth, the forester will recommend professional cutters and help you in assessing the bids these cutters will provide you for harvesting such timber. You can be assured that the cutters recommended by your county forester will be reliable. Without a starting point like this, you will be at the total mercy of the lumbermen. Some of them will not be trustworthy and you could face the risk of being ripped off if you try to do it yourself. You will be far better off seeking the kind of professional help your county forester can provide.

There are also private forestry organizations such as the New England Forestry Foundation. Their foresters will act as consultants for you and handle the entire process from beginning to end for a small percentage of the timber sale as their fee. This saves you a tremendous amount of paper work and time—not to mention the headaches!

CULLING THE WOODLOT

A woodlot needs to be culled. In nature, a herd or flock has its old, its infirm , its healthy, and its young. Predators and the laws of nature provide that the old and infirm make way for the young. When there is a proper balance, the herd thrives and there is constant strengthening of the herd because of it. A woodlot is no different! It, too, needs to have the old and infirm removed to make way for the young and the healthy. The only problem is in recognizing which trees need to be removed.

In looking over your woodlot, take particular notice of any trees that are large and especially straight for a distance of 16 or 20 feet. Such trees should be in excess of 16 inches in diameter at breast height (DBH). If you think you have a quantity of such trees, you can investigate the possibility of harvesting them for timber purposes. If you don't use the services of your county forester or a private forester, you can try to contact some local lumbering companies and let them provide you with a quote for harvesting the timber.

Be sure to get at least three quotes. But more importantly, check carefully to find out if the lumber cutters are reputable. Most importantly, get your money up front, not *after* the lumber is gone! Any reputable logger or logging company should be willing to pay you up front. If they are reluctant to do so, I would advise not dealing with them.

One further concern here is to get a firm contract with a performance bond that insures that the company will clean up the land to your satisfaction upon completion of the logging operation. Most state laws only require that such logging operators need clean up the slash within 100 feet of a public road. I don't feel the same should apply to a private operation. I would advise that you insist on a complete cleanup of the area. Of course, there will need to be a trade-off here because if you insist on a complete job the price the logger can offer you will be less. You'll have to decide the better way for you.

One thing you can do is to make some deal with the logger that will make the job of harvesting the tops for firewood easier for yourself. You can require them to pile all the harvestable firewood in one area and to deposit the brush in another area. Better still, try to get them to chip up the brush before they leave the area. Chipped brush will rot quickly and provide a valuable mulch for the forest floor. Otherwise, you will have to accept that they will spread the brush around and that it will take a few years for the brush to completely break down naturally and return to the forest floor.

After determining which trees are salable to a logging operation, the next step in management is to determine which trees can be taken out for sanitary purposes. These will be trees that are dead or dying, diseased, crooked, or growing in clumps. There are many ways to determine which trees should go in this second step. For instance, if a white pine tree is only 6 inches in diameter, but has a very furrowed bark, you can be fairly certain the tree has been stunted and should be taken out. White pine trees should not acquire a heavily furrowed bark until they reach some 12 inches in diameter.

Trees that are leaning heavily in one direction should be removed. This is especially true if they are leaning over a stand of younger trees and shading out their growth potential. Such a leaner will never really amount to much and it will die at an earlier age than a straight tree.

Look up into the canopy of the woodlot and try to pick out trees that have dead branches and are lacking in full-sized leaves. These are trees that should come out to make way for the healthier trees that need to replace them in the future. Look also for trees that are ringed with woodpecker holes. This is another indication of a tree that will not live out its usefulness.

Trees that grow in a "Y"—two from the same stump—or more than two, are prime subjects for rotting and disease. You should leave only straight, single trees that will grow into useful timber or good firewood specimens. The only exception to this would be your desire to leave occasional older trees with holes in them to serve as homes for wildlife.

Other trees that should be removed are the weed species. Depending on what part of the country you live in, certain species of trees can be considered weeds. In the Northeast, they are the sumacs, alders, poplars, ironwood, and such. They serve no purpose for firewood or timber and should be removed to make way for good firewood stands. A quick investigation with your forester or some other person knowledgeable about the area in which you live will help determine which trees are considered weeds.

MANAGING FOR WILDLIFE

Managing your woodlot can serve a dual purpose that can help make your land more pleasurable. By leaving the seed or nut bearing shrubs and trees intact, you can provide food for birds and other wildlife. Blueberries, shadbush, nut trees of many kinds, and other naturally occurring species can be left in your woods. It can be a real pleasure working your woodlot on a pleasant day in the company of the birds and small animals that are attracted to an area that has a good supply.

As you cut over an area, take a little time to plant some seed or berry bearing shrubs for the wildlife. Information about what species are best suited for your area and where to get them can be obtained from any number of sources. Your town seed store, as well as garden outlets and nurseries, will know what to suggest and will have some available. Most towns have a conservation commission that can make certain species of trees and shrubs available to residents, especially around Arbor Day each year. Local garden clubs have access to these plants too, and, if you are fortunate enough to have a local Audubon chapter nearby, they can certainly offer information about availability and even advice as to what, where, and when to plant.

Take a little more time to provide a water source for wildlife on your property. You will be assuring yourself a plentiful population of these pleasant creatures by providing a watering hole for them. Sure it might bring some mosquitoes in the summer months, but that will only assure you of more birds being attracted to a plentiful supply of insect life. In this respect, you will have to decide which is the better trade-off. Given the choice, I believe most of us will choose the natural route to a sterile landscape and we'll be doing something positive for the environment in the process.

IMPROVING THE STAND

After you have culled the large trees for timber, the diseased and infirm ones for sanitation, and have prepared the forest floor by removing a portion of the weed growth, you are ready to look around and select which trees you should remove for providing living space.

The best time to determine which trees should go for spacing is when leaves are on the trees. When you look up into the canopy of the forest, you should be able to see spaces between where one tree branch approaches another tree. Trees should be removed so that you allow light to the forest floor. In so doing, you will provide the sunlight that will enable the smaller, young trees to germinate and flourish. If they are continually shaded, they will grow slowly at best and might die before they amount to anything useful.

While you can prune softwoods and the branches do not grow back, hardwoods will sprout new branches even though they are pruned. However, I prefer to prune hardwood trunks as well as the conifers. In so doing, the forest is a more pleasant place to walk. I prune up to a height of about 8 feet. However I never prune more than two-thirds of any tree. Keeping the large branches off the main trunk of a tree makes it much easier to manuever in the woods. When the tree is dropped later on, it will be a simpler tree to buck up.

Firewood is becoming increasingly difficult to find, very valuable, and high-priced. In Vermont, it is estimated that about 500,000 cords of wood are being harvested and burned annually. That's a lot of wood and there is much concern that if we continue on this woodburning kick we will decimate our forests in a very short time.

However, there are offsetting arguments to this. I also recall reading that a large portion of the heating needs of the Northeast can be provided with just 10 percent of the renewable growth of trees in the Northeast! I am convinced that a huge part of our forests are not being properly managed to assure adequate supplies of firewood.

It has been estimated that nearly 60 percent of all forest lands are in the hands of farmers and private owners. Yet these lands produce less than half of our wood products. For lack of management, these acres are producing no more than a third to a half of what they are capable of yielding. By comparison, forest industry lands comprise only 14 percent of total forest area and produce 28 percent of all wood products.

I believe this assessment is conservative at best. Private lands in the Northeast produce far less than they are capable of producing. I further contend that the big fault lies in the ignorance of land owners and the apathy of government agencies to do anything about it.

I'll guarantee you that every town in New England, except possibly those in the heavily populated Metropolitan areas, have many acres of woodlands that are either being mismanaged or not managed at all. More than likely, no one has ever given thought to management of any kind. Many dump sites are surrounded by stands of trees, probably dying from the leachate of the dump! Town conservation commissions hold many more acres of woodland that are being held in a pristene way—hands off at any cost. A great many schools have woodlands surrounding them. Town tree-belts have overgrown trees and crowded stands that deserve management and thinning in many cases.

DISCRETIONARY CUTTING

In many of these examples, a very discretionary program of harvesting should be initiated. I am not advocating denuding our conservation lands or our schoolyards and such. I said *discretionary* cutting. It would take a lot of planning and even more supervision to properly do the job, but it can be done. We have work forces standing by just waiting to do the job of supervising—our Boy Scouts and Girl Scouts, our golden agers: any number of retired persons in a town: our garden clubs: our conservation commissions, rotary clubs, and many others. Given an opportunity to perform a civic duty in supervising cutting, I believe we could do a fantastic job in managing the woodlands every town has.

And what about the private owners who are doing absolutely nothing with their lands except allowing mature trees to stand dying or shading the young growth of their forests? Why not some kind of inducement to allow the populace to benefit from their lands? I'm still referring to supervised cutting with discretion. Everyone would benefit. The land owners would see their lands properly cleaned up and would receive compensation for this. Those of us who want to burn wood would have a source of heat

nearby. Best of all, we would be doing the country a favor by decreasing our dependence on conventional fuels.

Like most of you, when I drive throughout the countryside or even along the Massachusetts Turnpike, I see hundreds of square miles of trees that are being completely unmanaged. Some day we will wake to the fact that we cannot continue to allow this. Foreign nations have for years managed every square inch of their forest lands to the benefit of the landowner and the populace. We allow ours to waste away through neglect. But that is nothing new to the American people. We have wasted our resources for two centuries now. Can we change?

In closing, let me just state the definition of conservation, a movement I've been involved in for many years. This definition is seldom repeated or accepted. It is as follows: "Conservation is the wisest use of our resources."

Index

Edited by Steven Bolt